THE ABWEHR

THE ABWEHR

German Military Intelligence
in
World War Two

Lauran Paine

ROBERT HALE · LONDON

© Lauran Paine 1984
First published in Great Britain 1984

ISBN 0 7091 9628 8

Robert Hale Limited
Clerkenwell House
Clerkenwell Green
London EC1R 0HT

Photoset by Rowland Phototypesetting Ltd
Printed in Great Britain by
St Edmundsbury Press, Bury St Edmunds, Suffolk
Bound by Woolnough Bookbinding Ltd

Contents

List of Illustrations

1

The Evolution of Ideals

An English authority, Edward Caird, said Hegel's *Logic* was 'the one work which the modern world had to put beside the *Metaphysics* of Aristotle'.

Hegel dealt with the great concerns of human existence: the organization of society, the state, law and morality, art and religion.

A century before Adolf Hitler became Chancellor of Germany, in a course of lectures at the University of Berlin, Hegel expounded upon the role of 'World Historical Individuals', who were, he said, the agents through which the 'Will of the World Spirit' was made manifest.

'They may be called heroes,' he explained, 'in as much as they have devised their purpose and their vocations not from the regular course of things, sanctioned by the existing order, but from a concealed fount, from the Inner Spirit, still hidden beneath the surface, which impinges on the outer world as on a shell, and bursts it to pieces . . . They were practical, political men . . .'

According to Hegel, 'World History occupies a higher ground than that on which morality has properly its position, which is personal character and the conscience of individuals. . . . Moral claims which are irrelevant must not be brought into collision with world-historical deeds and their accomplishment. The litany of private virtues – modesty, humanity, philanthropy and forbearance – must not be raised against them.'

Conscienceless tyranny, then, was above the law.

'So mighty a form [as the World Historical Individual] must trample down many an innocent flower – crush to pieces many an object in its path.'

Hegel's companions-in-thought, Schopenhauer, Nietzsche and Wagner, sanctioned what a subsequent German of substance, Prince Bernhard von Bülow, would claim as fact after the turn of the present century: the right of a Germany which was authorized by Providence to be exempt from all ordinary laws governing human conduct, '. . . to trample down many an innocent flower – crush to pieces . . .' objects in its political path. In Hegel's Germany the seeds of a philosophy were planted which would bear perennial fruit.

Ninety-two years after Hegel's death the 'World Historical Individual' Adolf Hitler crushed Czechoslovakia and Poland. Ninety-three years after Hegel's death Hitler conquered France, Norway, Denmark, Belgium, Luxembourg and the Netherlands; he owned Europe.

In the rhetoric of a different era Hitler addressed the Reichstag in 1938 in these words straight out of Hegel: 'Above all, a man who feels it is his duty at such an hour to assume the leadership of his people is not responsible to the laws of parliamentary usage or to a particular democratic conception, but solely to the mission placed upon him. And anyone who interferes with this mission is an enemy of the people.'

The cant of German philosophers was solidly embedded in these words. But by 1939 to achieve the goals of such conviction required methods unknown in Hegel's day. The world was less susceptible to a mailed fist no matter how menacing, nor were men as illiterate or pliable even in Germany.

More than armies were required. Entire national populations of men, women, grown children and old people had to be indoctrinated. In conquered lands people could be subjugated, but in National Socialist Germany they had to be mobilized behind the ideals; they had to *believe*.

Nevertheless it was impossible to control all thought, all conviction, all conscience, therefore Germany had to be policed, and no nation of recent history with one possible exception was as thoroughly policed as was National Socialist Germany. Out of a population of approximately eighty million people, roughly eight million were involved in some form of control. Police authority extended to every phase of German existence. There were no exceptions, not even among the authorities themselves. There were police to watch leaders as well as police bureaux to spy on other police bureaux. There were agencies for internal as well as external espionage. All these organizations were ruled by ambitious men, none of whom acknowledged the superiority of other police-espionage agencies, and in the catastrophic closing years of the Second World War it became as hazardous for the Abwehr, the Military Intelligence organization, to exist in Germany as it was for Abwehr personnel to serve in France or Russia.

There was reason to believe the Abwehr could serve Germany's Third Reich without the odium which ultimately became synonymous with the other secret services because it was not a political bureau, as were the Shutz-Staffel (literally: 'Defence Echelon'), which achieved great notoriety through its initials, SS, or the Geheime Staats Polizei, the secret state police, best known by its abbreviation, Gestapo, or even the Sicherheitsdienst, or SD, the Nazi Party Intelligence organization.

Theoretically the Abwehr's position was one of unassailable prestige in re-armed Germany; it was the Intelligence Service of the Supreme Military Armed Forces Headquarters. Its duties were exclusively those of a professional Intelligence agency, and while this prevented it from becoming an instrument of the German National Socialist Workers (Nazi) Party, its function was to serve the nation, and the nation was ruled by Nazis.

The German term *Nachrichtendienst* implies 'Intelligence Service'. In fact there is no German word (or French word either, for that matter) which is an equivalent for the term 'Intelligence' as used among English-speaking people.

The term *Abwehr* corresponded to the English word 'Defence'. When used in context with the term *Nachrichtendienst*, it referred to an organization whose duty was to defend Germany; to counteract enemy – all foreign – Intelligence services. The Abwehr was particularly suitable to the situation of post-World War I Germany, a nation which was not to be allowed to think again in terms of offence, only defence.

According to the terms of the Versailles Treaty, defeated Germany was to be allowed to maintain a land force of 100,000 men, the Reichswehr or 'Defence Force'. In early 1921, when this organization was established, an Abwehr Intelligence bureau was created as part of the Ministry of Defence in Berlin. It was modest in size, consisting of about eight officers and a small clerical staff. It was divided into two divisions, East and West, and possessed no technical facilities, could not issue passports nor, originally, maintain a telecommunications centre, although it did maintain Intelligence stations at the headquarters of the seven military districts, each station under the supervision of one General Staff Officer.

The first Abwehr commander was Colonel Gempp, who had served in the First World War under the accomplished Prussian Colonel Walthar Nicolai, Chief of the Intelligence Service (Gruppe III b) of the Imperial General Staff. But in the 'thirties, with the advent of National Socialism, the re-birth of German nationalism and eventually the triumph of Adolf Hitler in his attempt to become German Chancellor, every bureau of the Defence Ministry was reorganized and enlarged. Colonel Gempp departed, to be succeeded by a naval officer, Captain Conrad Patzig, and a question which was to be repeatedly asked, arose. Why, since the Abwehr as staffed by Army personnel, and its function was to serve the Wehrmacht – 'Armed Forces', successor to the much smaller Reichswehr – was a naval officer chosen as its chief executive?

In Captain Patzig's case the reason was simply because after Colonel Gempp, and at the time of Patzig's appointment, the Abwehr was far too insignificant a bureau to interest ambitious Army officers. Later, after Patzig's departure, there appeared to be only one man particularly suited to supervise the intricacies of a rapidly expanding Intelligence agency and he also happened to be of the Navy.

Patzig's capabilities may not in any case have been adequate to organize what was clearly going to become in short order a very extensive secret service with worldwide contacts and networks.

Patzig was a blunt man of courage and ethics, attributes which inevitably brought him into conflict with Heinrich Himmler, Reichsführer of the SS, and also with Reinhard Heydrich, Himmler's chieftain of the SS Intelligence organization.

It was Himmler's complaints to the Minister of National Defence, Field Marshal Werner von Blomberg, which brought Captain Patzig into disfavour. Blomberg directed Admiral Erich Raeder, Naval Commander-in-Chief in 1935, to replace

Patzig on the grounds that the Abwehr chief was not acceptable to the National Socialist Party.

Raeder, whose natural affinities encouraged him to seek Patzig's successor among ranking naval officers, discovered that extremely few such officers possessed any of the qualifications to serve as a Chief of Intelligence at General Staff level. In fact at this time there was only one officer, Captain Wilhelm Canaris, shortly to be retired, who had the rank as well as the organizational experience to fulfil Raeder's requirements.

Wilhelm Franz Canaris was marking time at the sinecure of Swinemünde Fortress, a pleasant seaside resort on the River Oder facing the Baltic Sea, where he commanded a detachment of marines and a few coast artillery guns. Two years at Swinemünde was to be Canaris's last tour of duty before being retired with the rank of Rear-Admiral.

Nevertheless, and despite the lack of alternate choices, Admiral Raeder's decision was not a hasty one. He did not personally like Wilhelm Canaris, but more to the point Canaris's record suggested that he was likely to make judgements according to intuition more than logic. Nor was he a strict disciplinarian.

On the other hand, unless Raeder made the appointment, command of the Abwehr would certainly go to an Army officer, and in the competition among German armed forces, the Navy had never fared very well. It was therefore important not to relinquish this particular position.

Accordingly Admiral Raeder made the recommendation, and as of 1 January 1935 Captain Canaris replaced Captain Patzig as Chief of the Abwehr, but, because he had no Intelligence background, prior to the assumption of complete control Canaris spent a number of weeks familiarizing himself with the functions of an Intelligence organization.

It was a difficult time to learn a new trade. A year earlier the struggle for power in Germany had culminated in the murder of Ernst Roehm, head of the Nazi Brownshirts, and the ascendency of the generals, but within a few weeks President Paul von Hindenburg died and Adolf Hitler moved at once to assume the position of German President as well as Chancellor. By consolidating these positions under the new title of Führer, Hitler became ruler of Germany. Every member of the

armed forces, the Minister of Defence, the generals, were
required to swear a blood-oath of allegiance to Adolf Hitler
personally. This oath, possibly more than hallowed tradition,
would in the harrowing years ahead inhibit the only Germans
who could free Germany of the Nazi system, since the system
could only be overthrown providing Hitler were destroyed.

1935 was a period of considerable turbulence, not only in
Germany, where the industrial, social and commercial edifices
were in process of being Party-oriented, but also throughout
Europe, where the shadow of a stridently re-arming and
warlike Germany appeared as a menacing blight. 1935 was the
year conscription was reintroduced in Germany. In America it
was a year of widespread social unrest, the result of an earlier
economic collapse with ensuing unemployment, wholesale
bankruptcies, starvation wages and general disillusionment.
In Britain, where dedication to free trade had long been
weakening in favour of protective tariffs in an effort to support
the economy, unemployment and hardship were also widespread.

The West was struggling to find solutions to the most severe
economic stricture it had ever jointly experienced, and for any
leader to suggest rearmament as a counterbalance to German
ambition at a time when food was dear and guns were loathed,
would have been political suicide. Generally, even among the
French, whose country shared an extensive border with Germany, the foremost anxiety was over relief from the Depression, not rearming neighbours.

But the disintegration of international stability which had
proceeded rapidly with the onset of the Great Depression was
made to order for the ambitious man in Berlin, where the
economy which had been bolstered by infusions of foreign aid
since 1919, and was subsequently kept healthy through the
demands of rearming, was sound and flourishing. It was
inevitable that Germans who were employed and prosperous
would view the opposite conditions elsewhere as indications of
political and social decay, especially when an excellent Minister of Propaganda made a particular point of promoting this
viewpoint. It was also easy for Germans to accept the concepts
of flamboyant Nazis and their spartan leader whose orations
in defence of nationalism and Germany's rightful place among

powerful nations struck directly at the heart of Germany's humiliation after World War I, a sentiment which was still strong nineteen years after the surrender.

There were also a number of other encouraging reasons to support the new concepts. In May 1933 elections in the Free City of Danzig yielded thirty-nine out of seventy-two seats to the National Socialists. By June Nazi elements boring from within had achieved control of the government. On 14 October Nazi Germany withdrew from the League of Nations. On 12 November the Reichstag voted ninety-two per cent in favour of Nazi candidates, and on 26 January 1935 the first breach of the French defensive alliance occurred when Poland concluded a separate treaty with Hitler's Germany to become the first friend of Nazi Germany in eastern Europe, as she would also ultimately become the first major victim.

On 14 June 1934 Reichsführer Hitler met with Italian Premier Benito Mussolini to discuss mutual interests, and while the meeting was a failure, it pointed clearly in the direction of a conceivable and eventual alliance.

On 25 July Nazi elements engineered the *Putsch* in Vienna. On 13 January 1935 a plebiscite in the Saar resulted in a ninety per cent vote favouring reunion with Germany as opposed to union with France, and this event marked the beginning of German expansion. It was followed three days later by Hitler's renunciation of the Versailles Treaty, which was followed by increases in every department of the German armed forces including the Abwehr under its new chief executive, Wilhelm Canaris.

2

The Organization

In the days of the Reichswehr very little money was available for the maintenance of an Intelligence bureau, nor was such a bureau considered necessary by some staff officers, an attitude which sharply limited Intelligence operations in the years between wars.

When Wilhelm Canaris became Abwehr director, the agency was simply another small department of the Ministry of Defence – the Reichswehrministerium, which Hitler renamed Reichskriegsministerium, or Ministry of War. Its tasks up to that time had been to help in concealing the expansion of the armed forces from foreign Intelligence services, and to develop a surveillance system toward the East, primarily toward Poland.

Initially these assignments could be accomplished at nominal expense, but it eventually became apparent that a nation with something to hide, as well as a desire for military parity with its neighbours, required more than just a small and indifferently funded Intelligence establishment. If it was to procure exact and precise information respecting the armaments, disposal and number of divisions, and the procurement logistics, of its neighbours, it would have to be expanded in the personnel sector and funded accordingly.

The matter of concealment became less important as time passed, and by the year Hitler renounced the Versailles Treaty it had become impossible in any case. Germany's clear course of rearmament was by then an open secret. It had been known for some time that the Russians, Spanish and Dutch were abetting German rearmament. In fact one of the factors which favoured the appointment of Captain Canaris as Military Secret Service chief was his involvement with the illegal and clandestine supervision of submarine construction at foreign, mainly Dutch, shipyards.

It was also important that Canaris had wide-ranging foreign contacts. Under his aegis it was correctly assumed that German Military Intelligence would possess a cosmopolitanism no other German Intelligence Service had. The Abwehr could therefore be relied upon as an organization of defence, with a nucleus from which a much larger Intelligence agency could be developed, under a director who, while lacking in specific Intelligence training, nevertheless understood Intelligence goals with respect to national requirements.

As provider of information to the General Staff, the Abwehr was ideally positioned to become the foremost Intelligence department at the War Ministry. It could collect, collate and present vital information with greater facility than any other Intelligence establishment, none of which, such as the Gestapo or SD, had been created to operate outside Germany, although in Nazi Germany there certainly was no shortage of Intelligence organizations, and most of them at one time or another aspired to become genuine espionage establishments.

Among these agencies the complexity and redundancy at times achieved an apex of absolute confusion. And with the passage of time, as these bureaux attempted to cannibalize one another, the value of their work suffered in relation to the politicking of their directors. Gestapo Chief Reichsführer Heinrich Himmler, as well as Walter Schellenberg, the SS Standartenführer who succeeded Canaris as head of the Abwehr in 1944, consistently worked to undermine the Abwehr, while at the same time arduously spying on every other Intelligence agency and being spied upon in turn by the service arm Intelligence bureaux. Although none of the secret state police organizations was authorized to conduct any Intelligence activity within or against the Wehrmacht, this was a prohibition which Security Service (SD) director Reinhard Heydrich, a former naval officer dismissed the service for dishonourable conduct, chose to ignore. His infiltration of SD agents among the officer corps in order to bring the Army under control of the secret police brought forth complaints and ensured antagonism between Himmler's Intelligence apparatus and the Army, which never abated.

But the Abwehr under Wilhelm Canaris managed for several years to maintain a high degree of professionalism. At Supreme Command level it was directly responsible to the Chief of Staff. Separate subsidiary departments were also attached to the High Command of each service arm: Navy, Army and Air Force, each of which also had its own Intelligence units. There was also the Party Intelligence organization, originally founded exclusively for internal spying. The various police bureaux also maintained Intelligence units, as did the Foreign Ministry, foreign trade, overseas travel and commerce *Konzerns*; and after war came, each administrative command in occupied countries had an Intelligence department.

In 1938, after the dismissal of Field Marshal von Blomberg for his marriage to Erna Gruhn, his secretary who had a police record for prostitution – unearthed by Himmler and Heydrich and taken immediately to Hitler – and the abolition of the Ministry of Defence, the Abwehr was elevated to the position of Amtsgruppe (group of departments) attached to the Supreme Command of the Armed Forces – 'Oberkommando der Wehrmacht', abbreviated as OKW.

Abwehr Amtsgruppe consisted of five departments; foreign (*Ausland*) under Captain, later Vice-Admiral, Buerkner, whose duties did not include secret military Intelligence but rather relations with foreign powers, especially allied foreign powers. It was also to maintain liaison between the Supreme Command of the Armed Forces – the OKW – and the Ministry of Foreign Affairs. It was the department to which German military attachés overseas reported, and it was responsible for the procurement of information from abroad through secret channels.

Section I ultimately controlled a series of branch offices whose personnel created espionage networks and recruited V-men (*Vertrauensmann*: reliable informant). It was engaged in active espionage, upon occasion widespread counter-espionage, and through these sources accumulation of information concerning the war industries, the war-making potential, of neutral, friendly and enemy states.

It has been said that the Abwehr's function was concerned only with obtaining Intelligence to be presented to the pertinent agencies of war, Army, Navy, Air Force, as well as the Chief of Operations of the Armed Forces, and that Section I in particular was employed only in this fashion. But in fact

Section I maintained an extensive counter-espionage department which included vast underground networks throughout the Low Countries and France and for a time had agents in Britain whose functions went well beyond the simple accumulation of information.

Section II, under Colonel, later Major-General, Erwin von Lahousen, was concerned with sabotage and 'special duties', a term which was to cover a variety of undertakings as the war years advanced. Section II became one of the largest and most active departments of German Military Intelligence, as will subsequently be revealed.

Section III under Colonel, later Major-General, von Bentivegni, was responsible for counter-sabotage, counter-espionage and security. Its work, as also happened with von Lahousen's Section II, frequently overlapped areas of Gestapo involvement, particularly those of national security.

Each of the three principal sections had sub-sections which were concerned with co-operation with the service arms, Army, Navy and Air Force, with collection of economic and commercial information, and technical data, with forged documents for spies, wireless equipment, the organization of clandestine wireless units for internal defence, and foreign espionage.

The administrative section under Colonel, later General, Hans Oster, functioned solely as a bureau of archives, legalities and finance for the operational departments.

Section III, Security and Counter-Espionage, had its three sub-sections, III-H, Army, III-L, Air Force, and III-M, Navy, under another sub-section, Group III-W, which was responsible for exposing espionage in the three services, Army, Navy and Air Force, which, according to other regulations, no secret service agency was supposed to do.

There was also an Abwehr counterpart to the Intelligence (internal) departments of the SS, SD, Foreign Ministry and Party security bureaux, whose function was to spy upon and carefully investigate government officials and employees.

Also as part of Group III-W was a unit for surveillance of German industry, including security police, armaments inspectors, and factory and clerical personnel, which was a clear duplication of effort with the Gestapo.

Bentivegni's Section III had a Group III-D sub-section responsible for the dissemination of false and misleading information to foreign Intelligence services: 'black propaganda'. It worked closely with sub-section Group F, the counter-espionage unit charged not only with countering operations of enemy Intelligence services but also with penetrating them through implantation of Abwehr agents. It was also closely allied with Piekenbrock's Section I, active espionage, and von Lahousen's 'special duties' units.

Group III-G, also of Section III, had authority for investigating acts of sabotage and espionage, and advising the services respecting treason, sabotage and espionage by German nationals.

After the declarations of war two additional groups were added to Section III: Group III-KGF, responsible for preventing espionage and sabotage in prisoner-of-war camps, and Group III-N for the detection and prevention of sabotage in all areas of communication such as radio, telegraph and the postal service.

Also, by this time the Abwehr was re-designated the Department of Foreign Countries and Counter-Espionage at Supreme Armed Forces Headquarters. But it retained its independent status, being designed to serve all Wehrmacht services without being incorporated into any of them.

The expansion which had provided von Bentivegni's Section III with its diverse groups and sub-sections also provided Colonel Piekenbrock's Section I with an additional five groups. Group I (*Wirtschaft*) collected commercial and economic information. Group I (*Heerestechnik*), collected technical information for the Army. Group I (*Luftwaffentechnik*) collected technical information for the Air Force. Group I-G designed and supervised the construction of radio sets for secret agents and underground organizations, and also assisted and supervised the creation of radio networks for counter-espionage purposes.

Section II, von Lahousen, also acquired several sub-sections. Group II-H was to co-ordinate information acquired through the Section's 'special duty' personnel with the Army. Group II-M did the same for the Navy, and Group II-L performed the same service for the Air Force.

There was friction between the Gestapo and Section III's Group III-W Sub-Groups C-1 and C-2, the former involved with surveillance of government employees, the latter with surveillance and investigation of all other civilians except those engaged in industry. Friction also occasionally occurred between the Gestapo and von Lahousen's Section II, whose 'special duties' frequently impinged upon Gestapo areas of internal concern.

It is difficult to understand how there could *not* have been trampled toes, and not only with the Gestapo, except that Heydrich and Himmler were unwavering enemies of the Abwehr; they never overlooked an opportunity to denigrate it nor permitted a chance to slip by when they could contrive something derogatory about its chief.

But there was almost no friction between the services and the Abwehr despite consistent duplication especially in conquered countries where each military command had an *Abwehrstelle* (abbreviated AST), an Abwehr Intelligence station supervised by an IC A/O (IC meaning personnel of General Staff level who evaluated Intelligence, and A/O meaning Security Officer, or *Abwehroffizier*). These stations worked in close conjunction with armed forces Intelligence establishments.

Such service-attached stations were in operation when Canaris assumed Abwehr directorship, and he did little to change their organizational structure even after the war began, except to increase personnel. Basically, they were divided according to their duties to conform to Abwehr Headquarters divisions, Groups I, II, III, handling the responsibilities of Headquarter Sections I, II and III. i.e., collection of information, security services, espionage and counter-espionage, sabotage and 'black propaganda'. They also maintained forward units with advancing corps, operated border posts and established Intelligence echelons in sensitive or strategic areas.

At the onset of German action against Poland, on 1 September 1939 at 04.55 hours, Abwehr commandos advanced with the first invasion units, their purpose to seize Polish Intelligence personnel, protect advancing German regiments from the retaliatory activities of Polish security service troops, and capture classified documents.

By that time the Abwehr was a vast, complex, highly organized secret service no longer inhibited by lack of funds, although even then foreign exchange was not always available, except in instances of agents being assigned to foreign countries.

At its peak the organization consisted of fifteen thousand people. Such successes as the innovation of having armed personnel advancing with forward Wehrmacht elements was in later years to be copied by all Western powers. This system proved very satisfactory for Nazi Germany.

Piekenbrock's Section I established active and very productive espionage networks in France before the Allies were able to sort through the chaos to find suitable people for their own similar purpose.

If the Abwehr had a weakness in those early years, it was where foreign nations were concerned. The Germans could create adequate internal security, but because their foreign Intelligence services had not received support or full recognition, when war arrived in 1939 they had at best fragmentary and poorly organized Foreign Intelligence Organizations, often camouflaged as travel or trade companies, or, even more suspect, as scientific or diplomatic missions. For whatever these were worth, they were lumped under the designation 'Kriegsorganisationen', abbreviated as KO. In America, for example, where there had been no hostile German forces in over 150 years, and where Germany had no military aspirations, the Intelligence function was in the hands of amateurs. Even spies who were eventually sent to America were the worst examples of Intelligence people, and this emphasized another Abwehr shortcoming: training.

The German secret services never succeeded in creating an adequate training programme for spies to be sent into hostile countries which increased by one whit the chances for survival of agents whose chances would not have been good under any circumstances in this area, and with reason. Germany's spymasters – and some who were not spymasters, such as Adolf Hitler – had great respect for British Intelligence, without a question the best in the world. Nor did the Germans succeed in correcting these shortcomings, although between 1938 and 1945 they had eight years in which to do so.

There perhaps was mitigation. It did not excuse failure but it made it understandable. Germany in peacetime had never possessed a military police force. Even after war came, the Military Intelligence Service had no executive branch. It was a stepchild of the Armed Services and had to rely for police power on the normal police departments. But with the creation of the Gestapo and its policy of acquiring all national police and security power, the Abwehr was required to work through local police authorities, or through its enemy the Gestapo. When the latter course was necessary, the Abwehr was required to reveal its purpose, which invariably resulted in usurpation or bungling, the latter often the result of deliberate design.

Eventually, when the Gestapo undertook to broaden its organizational base by creating overseas political Intelligence networks, something Germany had never before possessed, encroachment upon Abwehr operations encouraged Himmler's *sub rosa* campaign to destroy the executive branch of Military Intelligence and incorporate what remained into his own expanding police establishment.

Therefore the Abwehr's earlier shortcomings, which in time might have been corrected – inadequate training of spies, and lack of development of a professional foreign espionage apparatus – were initially hampered by General Staff neglect, and later by powerful opposition from the chief of State Security Services, Reichsführer-SS Himmler.

But until Germany's internal situation deteriorated to the extent that Himmler's power matched that of the General Staff, the Abwehr under Wilhelm Canaris functioned well.

But detailing the organizational structuring of Military Intelligence hardly offers a fair view of Canaris's new Abwehr. For example, von Bentivegni's Section III had among its stations a palatial villa in France, formerly the property of the French-Jewish actor Harry Baur who did not survive the war, known as Abwehr St-Germain. Commandant was Sturmbannfürher (Major) Eshig, with a chronic nervous stomach. This station was responsible for counter-espionage activity throughout the entire area of north-western France. The staff varied in size but was never small. Under Major Eshig was Obersturmfürer (Lieutenant) Erich Borchers, who drank too much but in mitigation for his frequent gaffes was responsible for recruiting an army sergeant named Hugo Bleicher for Military Intelligence service. Bleicher succeeded in destroying the most productive Allied espionage-sabotage network in France, Inter-Allied. He very nearly succeeded in planting a German agent in Britain's Special Operations Executive counter-intelligence bureau, and in luring a British Major-General into Occupied France.

Abwehr St-Germain's successes were extensive. So extensive in fact that thirty years after the war had ended, British, French and American authorities still refused access to war-time files.

Some of these successes resulted from Abwehr St-Germain's policy of candid kindness. Many Allied agents were 'turned around' simply by having explained to them the alternative to co-operation with Military Intelligence – being handed over to the Gestapo. These double agents fed false information to the Allies, encouraged air-dropping additional secret agents into France where Germans were waiting, and extorted large sums of money, tons of armaments and the latest, most sophisticated wireless equipment for German use.

At Abwehr St-Germain they had a palatial parlour, a fine piano and luxurious bedrooms upstairs. Hugo Bleicher among other agents made full use of the inducements to recruit French nationals. Although Bleicher was an unprepossessing man, but persuasively cunning, one of Britain's best spies in France, Mathilde Carré, a green-eyed nymphomaniac, sang while he played the piano, then went upstairs with him, and in the morning Bleicher had won a mistress and a double agent who co-operated in identifying other Allied agents, many of whom died by firing squad or were incinerated.

There were equally as well-staffed Abwehr stations in Holland, Belgium, Denmark and Norway. In Istanbul, under station chief Dr Paul Leverkuehn, who was also director of what was called the Near East War Organization, the intrigues and politicking were endless, not only among spies of every shade and persuasion but also among the espionage agencies. SD agents spied on the Abwehr and in turn were also spied upon. Here, in the final years of struggle, occurred the defection of German agents – Dr Erich Vermehren and his wife, the former Countess von Plettenberg – which played an important part in bringing down the Abwehr. But in fact this was not an act of initial betrayal. Vermehren was a member of the Schwarze Kapelle, the secret organization within Germany which opposed Hitler. He had been in earlier contact with British Intelligence.

The SD also had a spy: Cornelia Kapp, daughter of a German diplomat, was the lover of the American military attaché in Ankara, George Erle. Part of her duties consisted of opening the morning mail. She '. . . handed over copies to the Americans every evening'.

But Kapp's double-agenting did not come to light until the SD's resounding success in the Cicero affair.

This incident, repeatedly chronicled in magazine articles and books ever after, in which the contents of the British Ambassador's safe were sold to the Germans – not the Abwehr but the SD and the Foreign Office – further detracted from the Abwehr's status. But each Abwehr station operated with almost complete autonomy, keeping Berlin headquarters informed of missions, but rarely details. If there was a failure, a defection or a missed opportunity, as occurred in the Cicero affair, a station might be at fault if it had independently initiated the activity or had neglected to seize an opportunity, but not headquarters.

The organization was huge. Never as large as the Gestapo but sufficiently large to preclude a possibility of the executive branch capably handling every detail of all affairs throughout Europe or the Middle East, Soviet Russia or North and South America. Nor could the directorship have properly handled activities in areas where only personal supervision might ensure competency. Nonetheless an Abwehr failure anywhere reflected against the man at 76/78 Tirpitzufer who directed the entire Military Intelligence organization, as well as supervised a secret conspiracy, and no one was more aware of this than Wilhelm Canaris, who successfully balanced for so long upon the edge of the sword.

3

Canaris

Misjudgements of pre-war Germany and its National Socialist leaders were common. In 1935 Winston Churchill stated in his book *Great Contemporaries* that Hitler's struggle to achieve leadership could not 'be read [about] without admiration for the courage, the perseverance, the vital force which enabled him to challenge, defy, conciliate or overcome all the authorities or resistance which barred his path'.

The last British Ambassador to pre-war Germany, Sir Neville Henderson, wrote in 1939 that, 'It would be idle to deny the great achievements of the man who restored to the German nation its self-respect and its disciplined orderliness . . .'

Shortly after Sir Neville's eulogy and for the ensuing thirty-five years no individual of conscience praised Hitler or any of the National Socialist hierarchy who served with him: Goering, Himmler, Goebbels, Rosenberg and the rest. In the light of subsequent history, Nazi leaders were categorized as the worst possible men. Their characters, their actions, their personal behaviour ensured this judgement during the war and into the future. Only two Nazis of the top echelon escaped general condemnation: Albert Speer, whose subsequent existence was dedicated to a masterful display of injured innocence, and Wilhelm Canaris, whose death during the last weeks of the war bequeathed a legacy of mystery and uncertainty which exists to this day and will never be resolved. While he lived he was an enigma. In death he remains one.

A contemporary who was equally as devious and secretive, General Sir Stewart Menzies, the grey eminence of the British secret service, whose life paralleled that of Canaris and whose death would also be tragic, said that Canaris was 'damned brave and damned unlucky'.

Ernst Kaltenbrunner, brutal chief of the Sicherheitsdienst – SD – Canaris's rival and enemy, said at Nuremberg: 'I have ascertained the high treason of Canaris to a most terrible degree.'

Allen Dulles, American spymaster in Switzerland and subsequently Director of the Central Intelligence Agency – who discreetly arranged for a pension for Canaris's widow – thought Wilhelm Canaris was 'one of the bravest men of modern history'.

The hulking, scar-faced SS leader whose wartime exploits read like fiction, Otto Skorzeny, said, 'Canaris betrayed his country's military secrets to Britain directly and wittingly from the beginning of his career to its end', and the wartime chief of Hitler's Intelligence evaluation organization, the Fremde Heere, General Reinhard Gehlen, who outlived nearly all of them, dying in 1979, said long after the war that Canaris's character was 'shrouded even now in mists of ill repute', while conceding that Canaris possessed 'Intellectual traits not seen in officers since the first half of the nineteenth century'.

An off-hand and superficial judgement was offered by a colonel of Britain's secret service, Samuel Lohan, who characterized Canaris as an 'inefficient, intriguing, traitorous, lisping queer'.

'Caudillo' Francisco Franco, who knew Canaris for more than twenty years – and who provided the villa in Spain for his widow – heeded his advice, enjoyed his company and trusted him absolutely.

Baron Ernst von Weizsäcker, Secretary of State at the German Foreign Ministry, who also knew Canaris well, wrote that Canaris was '. . . one of the most intriguing phenomena of the time, a type brought to light and perfected under dictatorship, a combination of disinterested idealism and shrewdness . . . He passed for a cunning Odysseus. This much even Hitler must have recognized, otherwise he would hardly have entrusted his whole military Intelligence to a sailor . . . Canaris had the gift of getting people to talk without revealing himself. His pale blue eyes did not uncover the depths of his being. Very seldom, and only through a narrow crack, did one see his crystal-clear character, the deeply moral and tragic side of his personality.'

He was a small man, five feet four inches tall, prematurely grey, who walked with his head slightly lowered, hands clasped behind his back, approachable, easy to spend time with, possessed of both a sense of humour and an uncanny intuition.

In many ways Canaris and Stewart Menzies were alike. Not in their private lives, but professionally. They were born within three years of each other; Canaris was the elder. Both served in the First World War. Afterwards, both became involved in affairs of national security, Menzies directly, Canaris indirectly, and both became Chief of Intelligence during the Second World War. Canaris was born on New Year's Day 1887 in the walled family residence at Aplerbeck, a suburb of Dortmund. His father was a man of substance in the mining and industrial community of Dortmund. Like Menzies's father, the elder Canaris – Carl – while not wealthy, was substantially well-off.

The mother of Wilhelm Franz Canaris, whose maiden name was Popp, was the daughter of the Master Forester of the Frankenwald holdings of the Dukes of Saxe-Coburg-Gotha. She was solidly German; her husband was not. Carl Canaris's forbears had migrated to Germany from Sala on Lake Como, the first being one Tomaso or Thomas Canarisi who, with several brothers, settled at Bernkastel as a vineyard worker. One forbear was named Giuseppe; another, Thomas or Tomaso, married the daughter of one Puricelli, another immigrant from Lake Como. Wilhelm's great-great-grandfather, Franz Canaris – they deleted the final letter 'i' about this time – became the *Kammerrat*, or Chamberlain, at the Court of the Elector of Treves. That was in 1789; they were then Catholics, but after the turn of the nineteenth century, with the Germanizing process well in progress, they became Protestants. Later Wilhelm's grandfather became mine master to the Dukedom of Hesse. His father, Carl, remained with mining and manufacturing. None of them had been soldiers or sailors, although there was a bare possibility that they were related to the Greek naval hero Konstantin Kanaris whose fireships vanquished the Turkish fleet of Kara Ali at Chios on 19 June 1822, a factor which contributed to Greece's liberation from Ottoman rule, and Konstantin's elevation as a Greek national hero.

It may have been this tenuous relationship with the redoubtable Greek which inspired Wilhelm to join the German Navy in the spring of 1905. He was an apt midshipman, good-natured, humane, efficient, and shortly before the outbreak of hostilities in 1914 he was appointed a junior officer aboard the light cruiser *Dresden*, scheduled for duty in the South Atlantic. The *Dresden* was refuelling in the Dutch West Indies when war was declared. The ship set course at once for Allied sea lanes where she operated with great success against merchant vessels seeking to supply Great Britain from Central and South American ports. At the Battle of Coronel in October 1914 she fought prominently as part of Admiral Graf Spee's German flotilla which destroyed the British squadron of Admiral Sir Christopher Caddock. Later, at the Battle of the Falkland Islands, the *Dresden* was the only German warship to survive. Eluding British pursuit by high speed, *Dresden* managed to remain alive one hundred days, hiding, sailing by night, short of fuel and food, and when she was eventually resupplied, with her back to the black lava island of *Mas a Fuera* in the territorial waters of Chile, three British cruisers trapped her.

HMS *Glasgow*, the only British warship to have survived Coronel opened fire, and Flag Officer Lieutenant Wilhelm Canaris put off from *Dresden* to parley. But this was not his sole purpose. *Dresden*'s Captain, Commander Ludecke, was preparing to scuttle and needed time. The sea cocks were opened and a charge was set, then the crew was sent ashore.

Lieutenant Canaris told *Glasgow*'s officer that *Dresden* was in neutral waters and that *Glasgow*'s attack was a contravention of international naval conventions. The Englishman's reply was blunt: 'I have orders to destroy the *Dresden* wherever she may be. After that matters can be settled by the British and Chilean diplomats.'

The demolition charge holed the *Dresden*; the explosion still echoed when Lieutenant Canaris saluted, went aboard his small boat and was rowed ashore to join the German crew in singing the national anthem while *Dresden* sank with battle pennants flying.

The Chileans interned *Dresden*'s crew. The wounded were

sent to Valparaiso for care; the others were sent into captivity at Quiriquina Island, five hundred miles out in the Pacific.

Canaris had a gift for languages and during duty in the Southern Hemisphere had learned Spanish. It helped him convince a Quiriquina fisherman to take him to the mainland. It also helped that he offered the Chilean a bribe.

At the German Embassy in Santiago Lieutenant Canaris was supplied with funds and a forged passport in the name of Reed-Rosas, an Anglo-Chilean. By automobile he reached the town of Osorno. From there, in the disguise of a Chilean peasant, he crossed the Andean *cordillera* afoot and on horseback, and reached Buenos Aires in Argentina thin as a rail and bothered by bouts of malaria, his Chilean passport intact and convincing.

Canaris was an excellent actor as well as an accomplished linguist. It helped that his size was unimpressive and his intuition perfect. As the Chilean widower Reed-Rosa *en route* to England to collect an inheritance left by a non-existent English mother, he boarded the Dutch Lloyd Line's SS *Frisia* bound for Rotterdam.

Nearing Europe, *Frisia* was overtaken by a British warship and ordered to put in at Plymouth, where British security authorities screened crew and passengers for German nationals. Several people were detained, but Canaris reached Rotterdam without further incident. His capacity for persuasion was tested when Dutch border guards were reluctant to allow a Chilean to leave Holland and enter Germany, but two days later he arrived in Hamburg at the residence of his aunt, Dorothea Popp, and on 17 September 1915 he reached the *Admiralstab* in Berlin, suffering from malaria and enteritis, exhausted and thin.

He was awarded the Knight's Cross, promoted to Captain and, after a period of leave to recuperate, assigned to the staff of Captain Kurt von Krohn, director of Germany's secret Intelligence and supply organization – Etappe – in Spain. In early 1916 he was in Madrid. Here, Stewart Menzies and Wilhelm Canaris were to have their only personal association. Here too, 'spies and assassins, double-dealers and feline deceivers marched four abreast down the long ramps of . . . political machinations.'

The secret war was being fought in neutral nations, while elsewhere torrents of blood ran in battle. At Loos British soldiers had captured 3,000 Germans at a cost of 60,000 casualties. A half million British soldiers were in France in 1916. At Verdun 281,000 Germans fell and 315,000 French died. The Somme was worse: 420,000 British casualties, 194,000 French, 440,000 German. One million dead, 40 French villages, dotted over 200 square miles, blotted out, and the war would not end for another two years. In one day in one battle Britain sustained 60,000 casualties. It was impossible to exaggerate the stakes in this conflict. They were not all upon the checkerboard battlefields of France, but that was where sickening statistics exemplified the kind of war it was.

In Madrid, Imperial Germany's clandestine undertakings heightened an atmosphere which was already dominated by every variety of political and military espionage. Excepting Basle, Madrid offered Germany her best view of conditions in the hostile world of Entente nations. Germany's military attaché in Madrid, Kalle, supervised a large network of spies while the naval attaché simultaneously maintained a successful surveillance of Allied naval flotillas. At stake was control of the Mediterranean and the Suez Canal, dominance of the Persian and Arabian oil estuaries, and, for Britain, the lifelines with her empire east of Suez.

German U-boats, operating with terrible accuracy against Allied shipping from the port of Pola in the Adriatic, had their courses established from information supplied by Captain Canaris to the German naval attaché. Canaris's duty had nothing to do, directly, with espionage. He was to recruit seamen along the docks who could gather information from seamen of neutral nations concerning schedules, courses and observations relative to every Allied sea function. He also created a network of informants among chandlers and others engaged in supplying shipmasters, and as the organization grew, it included men and officers of Spanish coast-wise vessels who frequently encountered Allied warships at sea, most of which were British. This information reached U-boat commanders from Captain Canaris through the embassy naval attaché.

Canaris operated as a civilian, the Anglo-Chileño Reed-

Rosas. It had been a successful disguise in Plymouth, but in Spanish-speaking Madrid no one speaking Spanish whose mother-tongue was German fooled anyone, and Britain's secret service had its own methods of successful penetration.

But Canaris's aptitude for this variety of clandestine employment went beyond creating an efficient information service. He was careful to maintain his own anonymity, moved frequently from hotel to private residences and used disguises, secret codes and mail-drops.

These were providential ruses, for, while Canaris did not know it, British agents in Madrid had picked up the trail of a German naval officer who was supplying the German Embassy with information which resulted in great damage to Allied shipping, and in the summer of 1916 an agent was sent to Spain to 'kill or capture' Canaris. The agent's name was Stewart Menzies.

But the options available to a British assassin in Spain were limited. King Alfonso, while a professed neutral, inclined towards the Central Powers. In general, Spaniards favoured Germany. Canaris liked Spaniards and made many friends among them, including men who would twenty years later be Spain's leaders. One was an enterprising Galician realist with a distaste for pomp. A man of wit and cunning: Francisco Franco.

Another factor intervened to hamper the assassins efforts. Canaris's health was deteriorating again. He worked too hard, something he did all his life, at times sleeping on a cot in an office for four hours a night then working with great intensity for twenty hours without rest. The bouts of malaria recurred. He needed medical treatment, but most of all he needed rest. Reluctantly Captain von Krohn inaugurated the orders for Canaris's return to Germany, but there was no safe way to reach Berlin from Iberia. Returning by air was out of the question. Going by sea was almost as hazardous. Disguised as a monk, complete with breviary, cowl and his Chilean passport, Wilhelm Canaris entered France as a pilgrim bound for the shrine of St Francis of Assisi. He safely crossed France to Italy, bound for the border town of Domodossola.

Allied counter-intelligence lost contact for a while but was again on the trail by the time Canaris reached Italy. Tracking a monk with a Chilean passport was not difficult, once the disguise had been penetrated. Italian authorities were alerted, and just short of the Swiss border Canaris was captured and jailed.

He was ill and exhausted, thin and pale, clearly a sick man. During interrogations he was embarrassed by fits of coughing which resulted in bloody expectoration, caused, he told the Italians, by terminal tuberculosis. To produce the blood he bit the inside of his mouth.

The Italians said he would be tried as a spy and probably sent to the wall. In Spain energetic protests moved the Italian Ambassador to inform his government that news of Canaris's imprisonment had aroused a storm of indignation in Madrid's diplomatic and governing circles.

The 'dying' German was released, the Chilean passport was returned, and while the Italians were relieved to be rid of a situation they had not been happy about, they were quite willing to co-operate with Allied Intelligence to the extent that they put Canaris aboard a Spanish ship bound for Genoa by way of Marseilles. Any German, but especially a German once accused of espionage, would never leave Marseilles alive, and of course the French authorities knew he was coming.

They waited in vain.

On the high seas Canaris went to the quarters of the Spanish sea captain. He was not, he said, a Chilean named Reed-Rosa; he was a German naval officer in poor health seeking to return home. If the ship put in at Marseilles where the French were waiting, he would be taken off, tried by court-martial and shot.

The Spaniard's gallantry had been appealed to. He responded by setting a fresh course for Cartagena, and after all those weeks of riding and walking, crossing through France and Italy and having Switzerland in sight, Wilhelm Canaris arrived in August back in Spain at the residence of Captain von Krohn, an ambulatory skeleton. But the assassin was getting closer; when the Spanish ship had failed to arrive at Marseilles, it was tracked to Cartagena, where, obviously, its passenger had headed inland where his contacts were. The pursuit, too, had come full circle.

Krohn wirelessed the Admiralty in Berlin for a U-boat to

pick up his ailing aide. Menzies knew by this time where his target was hiding. Juan March, a Spanish Jew, told him. Juan March was in 1916 a leader of Spanish port workers. Years later he would control Spain through its purse-strings. His sources of information were always reliable and almost infinite.

Also, von Krohn's message to Berlin had been intercepted by the British Admiralty's cryptanalytical section. A trap was arranged whereby both Captain Canaris and a German U-boat would be destroyed off Cartagena. Two French submarines, *Opale* and *Topaze*, were dispatched to lurk off Cartagena within sight of Tinoso Beacon.

In Berlin, the Admiralty dispatched the *U-35* whose Commander, Captain Arnauld de la Perière, was the German U-boat ace of the Mediterranean. Perière, like many Germans with singularly un-German names, was of French descent.

Menzies, with the aid of Juan March and accompanied by a British counter-intelligence team, went to Cartagena to supervise activities of three surface ships and a squadron of torpedo aircraft sent to support the brace of French submarines. They knew which U-boat was coming and where it would surface – in Salitrona Bay.

Canaris arrived at Cartagena and went aboard the interned German ship *Roma*. There were two additional Germans aboard *Roma*, also to be evacuated aboard the *U-35*. Later, in total darkness, they went aboard a Spanish fishing boat.

It had to be a dark night, the Spanish coastguards had to be diverted, and by now Canaris knew that Allied agents were in pursuit. At 02.30 hours on 1 October *U-35* raised periscope and found itself in the midst of fishing boats. One was supposed to be showing the Morse letter 'M' from its topmast. All the little boats had masthead lights. Captain de la Perière's quandary was not resolved until 06.32 when the black night was yielding to red dawn. He saw the letter 'M' and a red pennant and broke water without a sound beside the fishing boat; three night-shrouded wraiths sprang aboard and disappeared below; *U-35* silently sank and set course for Pola in the Adriatic. As a blazing sun arose to blind the periscope-watch of the *Opale* and *Topaze*, Wilhelm Canaris was on his way home, finally.

He underwent prolonged medical treatment in Germany and had a deserved long rest, then, at his request, was sent into training as a U-boat officer. In 1917 he was assigned to the fleet as a submarine commander. By the end of the war he had sunk eighteen enemy vessels.

Then came the collapse, the imposition upon Germany of merciless terms, revolution and anarchy, and Wilhelm Canaris the monarchist sought to find a balance in a world abruptly full of Bolsheviks and radical Socialists. Like many German officers, he had to await the return of order in the late 'twenties and early 'thirties before surfacing again as a strong national-ist.

But there was another side of the coin. Canaris was at least to some extent involved in the establishment of an Intelligence network throughout the Balkans, France, Italy and Germany in association with the British secret services. That is all that is known or probably ever will be known of this episode of his life. He was not an agent himself. That can be ascertained by his personal activities at this time. Later, when the Canaris itinerary was available for examination, it showed that he served prosaically as first officer of the cruiser *Berlin*, then as first officer of the antiquated battleship *Schlesien*, married the sister of a fellow officer, Erika Waag, became a naval lieuten-ant commander and, although involved with several right-wing organizations, was never so far as is known actively engaged in the violent episodes subsequently alleged. It was, for example, charged that he was implicated in the murders of two revolutionaries, Karl Liebknecht and Rosa Luxemburg, Bolshevik agitators whose leftist politics had earned them the antagonism of several nationalist groups, but while it was obvious that Canaris was a strong anti-Bolshevik, his accusers in this instance did not know their man: Canaris never con-doned murder or assassination. Later, in this respect, he would refuse to obey Hitler's orders. He was, as von Weizsaker and Allen Dulles said, an anachronism from the era of chivalry. He was religious and moral and often professed belief in a Law of Retribution from which neither individuals nor nations could escape.

He was a German patriot but never blindly so. Unlike other Germans coming to power in the 'thirties, Commander Canaris had travelled widely, had lived abroad, spoke several languages – French with least ease – knew and understood people, and believed in a destiny for Germany based upon restraint and freedom from the restrictions of the Versailles treaty. He was not a militarist in the German sense of that word, while he was simultaneously secretive and incorribly addicted to intrigue and, with a high degree of intelligence, managed to live with the alien components of his personality through times which drove similarly motivated Germans such as General Ludwig Beck to an early death fragmented in mind and body, or to the choice of assassination or suicide as with Erwin Rommel and others.

His unswerving purpose was to preserve Germany. Every subsequent action of his career was in the service of this one ideal, and in order to achieve this goal neither murder nor assassination was required.

But service aboard the *Schlesien* was simply a matter of passing time. Even when he became Commander. He served more than two years on the old warship, was appointed to the staff of the North Sea Command and at forty-three years of age had reached, and passed, the apogee of his naval career. The old knight von Beneckendorf und von Hindenburg was President of the Republic, Adolf Hitler was Chancellor, nationalism was on the march, and the clandestine part Commander Canaris had played in Holland, Spain and elsewhere in supervising the construction of Germany's new Navy gave substance to the conviction among Germans that the nation was no longer liable to the punishing restrictions of Versailles.

But Wilhelm Canaris was nearing retirement age. His assignment to Swinemünde was to precede separation from the service. He had watched Hitler's progress, questioned National Socialist methods and as completely misread Adolf Hitler as the Reichsführer was to misread Wilhelm Canaris. He approved of rearmament, particularly with respect to the new German fleet, approved of Germany's strong economy and believed that the Generals could control Hitler, oust him if necessary, so when the Abwehr appointment came, it is unlikely that the choice between well-earned retirement and ease, or a new and demanding career, entered Canaris's mind. The nation was freeing itself of the shackles imposed a decade and

more earlier. He had worked toward that freedom and pas-
sionately believed in it. As alluring as retirement appeared,
being part of new Germany's progress toward re-assuming
a position as a world power would have been irresistible,
and although Canaris was white-haired, he was strong and
healthy, in better condition now than he had been when he
had served the nation in 1914–18.

As for the position, he was confident. He knew little of the
details, but of Intelligence itself he understood enough. At his
first meeting with Hitler at the Reichskanzlei, when the Führer
said, 'What I want is something like the British Secret Service –
an organization doing its work with a passion', Canaris could
not have agreed more. As for the man now leading the German
state, Canaris, the polished manipulator of men, certainly felt
capable of succeeding here also.

But there could just as easily have been another reason.
Canaris was not a Nazi and had doubts about Hitler's immediate subordinates of the inner circle, many of whom, such as
Keitel and Jodl, he had known over the years. He may have
foreseen events. If so, he was not the only one.

It is possible that he accepted the Abwehr appointment in
order to frustrate where possible what appeared (to others as
well) to be Germany's headlong rush toward a devastating
destiny.

An Abwehr officer of the naval branch told American
Intelligence interrogators after the war that Canaris began
conspiring against the Nazis as soon as he assumed Abwehr
control. This was Captain Franz Maria Liedig, the least known
of Canaris's confidents. He said, 'The Canaris group within
the Abwehr was the first united military clique working
against Hitler with any semblance of a planned programme . . .
this . . . rebellion existed for many years before the war; it
actually began in 1934 when Admiral Canaris was put in
charge of the Abwehr.'

There were a few blind-loyal followers of Canaris such as Dr
Leverkuehn who refused to believe this, and it does not help
that those in Britain's Intelligence organizations with full
knowledge of these matters have maintained an obdurate
silence.

Others, including the Americans – who spirited away all the

Abwehr files they could find – the French and post-war Germans, have been less intransigent. But that still leaves a gap. Nonetheless, enough has come to light to suggest that Canaris's purpose never wavered. He wished to preserve the nation, that and that alone seemed to matter to him, but exactly *when* he became anti-Nazi is very much open to question.

4

The Intelligence Façade

One of the most bizarre characteristics of Spionage Abwehr was the way it successfully functioned as an Intelligence service, providing the OKW with information about the nation's enemies, while under the directorship of a man who by 1936, and perhaps earlier, had become more than simply a passive anti-Nazi.

But the man who became Abwehr chieftain in 1934 had served Germany as an ardent nationalist all his mature life. Early on he had disagreed in principle with Nazi methods but not with Hitler's objectives of reorganizing the nation, rearming it, advocating and implementing German equality.

By the time he was in a position to know the extent of Nazi atrocities not as rumour but as fact, he was Abwehr director. By then he knew more of Hitler's plans than any German who was excluded from the hierarchy of leadership. In his view they were suicidal. He was not alone in this sentiment; a number of prominent soldiers of the General Staff felt the same way. Even that incorrigible predator Hermann Goering argued against war in 1939. He believed Germany would not be ready to fight until 1941. He also believed that a war undertaken in 1941 must end in 1943. Nor did he favour an invasion in the east. He advocated attacking Spain, then with lightning swiftness fanning out with a series of conquests across the periphery of Mediterrania.

Had Hitler listened, the war could have lasted much longer than it did.

Canaris's reaction to either plan, that of the Reichsführer or the Reichsmarschall, was to categorize both as absolute madness, given the limits of the nation's economic power and armed might. He undertook to dissuade where he could, and to thwart where dissuasion failed. In his own words, he would 'do nothing to prolong this war by one day'.

31

The horns of the dilemma for a man in Canaris's position were elemental, and agonizing. He was an individual in whom nationalism had been paramount for decades. Simultaneously he was unalterably opposed to another German war of aggression. If he had been a Japanese, he could have resolved the issue by ritually sitting down and disembowelling himself.

His decision was to serve Germany as its military spymaster, at the same time seeking ways to end the war and depose the man and the system responsible for it. He would be loyal to the nation, its armed forces, its people and its historic institutions while working as best he could against the Austrian corporal and his sycophantic intimates. And because an Intelligence service 'is the ideal vehicle for a conspiracy', no one in Germany was in a better position to accomplish both goals, nor, it appears, was anyone as capable; Canaris was by nature a plotter, and a very talented one.

Also, dissent was by no means rare. Many Germans of substance and authority in trade and industry, as well as in the armed forces, watched with alarm as Hitler progressed steadily closer to the ultimate gamble. General Ludwig Beck, responsible for creating the new German Army, told Hitler to his face that the Führer's course would ruin the country, and that he had not modernized the Army for offensive conflict.

Others, dissident to the core, would have liked to have faced Hitler, but never did. The resistance was there, but it was fragmented. Among the Generals pessimism might prevail but there were two reasons why they remained loyal. One reason dated from the first week of August 1934.

Old Field Marshal von Hindenburg died on his camp bed, another relic of Tannenberg, at nine o'clock on 2 August 1934, a Bible in his hands. At three o'clock the Great General Staff was ordered to parade before the Column of Victory (the Siegessäule). At the same time Chancellor Adolf Hitler proclaimed himself Führer and directed the armed forces to swear allegiance. This was the hallowed blood-oath of Teutonic Knights – but with a difference.

Cannon fired in homage to Hindenburg, a band played the mournful '*Ich hatt' einen Kameraden*', the dirge of remembrance, and the Generals waited. After two minutes of silence, led by the Army's Commander-in-Chief (at that time Werner von Blomberg), a Bible in one hand, a national flag in the other hand, the Generals stepped forward to recite: 'I swear by God and this holy oath that I will render to Adolf Hitler, Führer of the German nation and people, Supreme Commander of the Armed Services, unconditional obedience, and I am ready as a brave soldier to risk my life at any time for this oath.'

The *Fahneneid* had been sworn to the person of Adolf Hitler, not to the nation.

After the ceremony Generals von Fritsch and Beck were leaving the Siegessäule when Beck abruptly halted and said, 'He took us completely unawares. I did not realize we were swearing a completely new kind of oath . . .'

These were men of the Wilhelminian period, soldiers of an earlier era and a former great war. To each of them an oath was sacred, and this particular oath would haunt every one of them for the rest of their lives. For Admiral Canaris it would create an obstacle he would never be able to overcome. Later generations would have had no difficulty disavowing allegiance gained through duplicity, but these German officers did not belong to any generation but their own. When the war began five years later, they suffered agonies but they did not break their oath.

That oath and Hitler's earlier courtship of the Generals, which resulted in eventual domination of, and contempt for, the General Staff, prevented an uprising among the only men who could have overthrown Hitler.

For Canaris these conditions left a single alternative. He had to create his organization, including the clandestine part of it, very carefully, and alone. In this he was abetted by the circumstances which occasioned Germany's need for a large and far-flung Intelligence establishment. With armed forces expansion, men entered the service who had no personal or family tradition as soldiers. There were also reactivated former officers, most of whom had served in the 1914–18 war, but had not served since. Each was classified as an E-Offizier, meaning a 'supplementary' officer. They were generally patriots of unquestioned loyalty to the *Nation*. Their politics were often, but not always, tainted with Nazi leanings. They were, however, more likely to have some political opinion than the professional German officers, who were singularly apolitical.

E-Officers commonly had the Old Army's prejudices; a good many of them were monarchists. They had learned soldiering under the old imperial system, which meant that, whether they were Nazis or not, they had been trained to accept German national policy without questioning it.

Ultimately Canaris had to include E-Officers among Abwehr personnel, but he was careful where they were assigned.

As for the civilians, the lawyers, architects, tradespeople, teachers and such who came into the service, few of whom possessed inherent loyalty to the military system, many of whom wholeheartedly detested it, a process of careful screening allowed selection of the best for Intelligence work, for, unlike the Army, Intelligence recruitment could result in rejection of a man who was physically capable but who was considered temperamentally unsuitable. Many Abwehr recruits were acquired from this manpower source. These 'Third Reich' officers were frequently men of independent spirit. Many were not Nazis, and there was considerable scepticism among them.

The screening process enabled Canaris to retain for Headquarters service individuals whom his nearly infallible intuition convinced him were not likely to be dedicated Nazis. Equally as talented people who *were* Nazis were usually assigned to Abwehrstelle (AST) units or to the increasing number of Abwehr sub-headquarters organizations in conquered countries. For purely political reasons some of these pro-Nazis were also assigned to the various Abwehr facilities within Germany. The Munich office for example was largely staffed by them.

Abwehr leadership, the executive branch consisting of section-heads, evolved from a patchwork nucleus which Canaris acquired either through inheritance from his predecessor Captain Patzig, or through recommendations and his own intuition.

One officer Admiral Canaris inherited and for whom he formed an enduring friendship was Major Hans Oster, Chief of Central (administrative) Section. Oster was a cavalry officer whose roots went back to the Imperial Army. Politically he was a monarchist, as much as he was anything. He was a vigorous, slender, at times rash man who deplored Hitler and detested Nazis. He had served briefly in the '100,000 man army', the Reichswehr, had been separated from the service and had returned as an E-Officer in the mid-thirties. Like Canaris, Hans Oster held convictions more common among German officers of the nineteenth century than of twentieth; he had a high sense of honour, abhorred corruption, was contemptuous of politicians and, when Nazi excesses became not isolated instances but a deliberate part of government policy, Oster often, and not very prudently, denounced them.

He was a serious man, observant, practical and realistic. At times he was also impatient and imprudently vocal. In character he and Canaris were quite similar, but in personality they were as different as night and day. Oster was outspoken. Canaris never was. Oster became directly involved. Canaris devised, planned and organized but rarely became physically involved. But they collaborated with complete confidence and ease. An officer who knew both men during the war afterwards said that identical motivation actuated them both. 'It was not political but ethical considerations which determined their acts.'

A rather different variety of individual was Colonel Piekenbrock, Chief of Abwehr Section I, a good-natured, outgoing Rhinelander, bluff, hearty, keenly intelligent, whose geniality masked hatred of Hitler and the National Socialists. Piekenbrock and Canaris were close friends. Piekenbrock called Canaris 'Excellency', half in humour, half in sarcasm. In the Old Army, general officers had been entitled to that designation.

Chief of Abwehr Section III, Staff-Colonel von Bentivegni, despite an un-German sounding name, had been born at Potsdam into a Prussian family with a substantial military background. Like Piekenbrock and Oster, von Bentivegni had served in the '100,000 man army'. He was older than the others, stiff and typically Prussian. He was meticulous about his personal appearance, even to the extent of affecting a monocle. But von Bentivegni was highly trained and Teutonically efficient, and he was no caricature of the Wilhelminians, even though he looked the part.

He was never as close as Canaris as were the younger

officers, and after the war it was said of von Bentivegni that he disapproved of the Admiral's anti-Nazism, but that is improbable. He served Canaris with total loyalty throughout the war, and earlier, until Canaris's dismissal as director in 1944, a very long time to disapprove of something without doing anything about it.

Bentivegni was a dedicated Intelligence officer. After the Admiral's removal he continued as a Section Chief of the Abwehr, and when the organization was incorporated into Himmler's National Security Organization (Reichssicherheitshauptamt), von Bentivegni was for a time acting director of all former Abwehr sections. Certainly he knew what was worth knowing at Abwehr headquarters. And as a collaborator of the Admiral in so many of the secret services which occupied the organization during the war, he could hardly have avoided being aware of the secret behind all the other secrets. It would have been impossible for him not to have known, if for no other reason than because of Hans Oster's candour at the Kalonnes, the staff ('Column') meetings.

Canaris's most promising acquisition, by way of the recruitment and screening process shortly before the war, was an Austrian, Erwin von Lahousen, a former member of Austria's 'K and K Army' ('Imperial and Royal', the old Austro-Hungarian Army). After the Anschluss of 1938, when Austria's secret service became part of the German Intelligence network, von Lahousen was recommended to Canaris by the Munich chief of the Abwehr station, Count (Graf) Morogna-Redwitz.

Lahousen was a former staff officer of the Austrian Army – the Bundesheer: or Federal Army. He had attended the Kriegsschule, ('School of War'), the equivalent of Germany's Kriegsakademie. He and Canaris had met briefly before annexation but not since.

Unlike other Abwehr executives, von Lahousen was neither a draftee nor an E-Officer. He had more in common at least in this respect with von Bentivegni. He was a professional soldier. He was also an aristocrat. Like Piekenbrock he possessed independent means and was not required to live on his salary as a Staff Colonel.

Lahousen was a linguist, an authority on the Balkans, a man who spoke quietly, never hastily. He was bald, tall (at Head-quarters his nick-name was 'Long L'), walked with a stoop, was good-natured and likeable and, despite impressive decora-tions, was unprepossessing even in tailored uniforms. He was far too cosmopolitan an Austrian ever to become a German Nazi. Admiral Canaris trusted him implicitly and relied upon his judgement and his efficiency, something he was never able to do with his chief of Foreign Section, Captain Buerkner, whom he had known at Wilhelmshaven. He once described Buerkner was a 'true-blue seaman and a rose-red optimist'.

It was accurate. Buerkner held an unalterable conviction of Germany's eventual triumph. He further believed that neither Himmler nor Heydrich was seriously in opposition to Canaris or the Abwehr, which was irritating enough, but Buerkner was also an inefficient department head, something the Admiral could not abide. But he was personable and loyal. He was an old friend. These things mattered with Canaris. He tolerated Buerkner when he knew better. It was this unique part of Canaris's character which later led analysts of the Admiral to say he was not really a good judge of men. He *was* a good judge; he simply never overcame feelings which were in-appropriate in a director of Intelligence, or, for that matter, a director of any large organization.

However, this flaw, if that is what it was, did not extend beyond the people he trusted most. His station chiefs, liaison officials, AST executives (officers assigned to those Abwehr units attached to field military commands), clerical, linguistic, strategic and technical people whose recruitment had been based entirely upon personal qualifications stated without exception that Admiral Canaris demanded maximum per-formance and would accept nothing less. A tireless worker himself, he expected a similar dedication in others.

If it was incredible that Canaris could simultaneously create a large, successful espionage system for the purpose of aug-menting German conquests, while secretly opposing the lead-ership which planned those conquests, the key to understand-ing such behaviour was the man himself, and if that might ameliorate the facts without quite explaining them, it did not alter a condition which existed. Canaris very carefully con-

structed his organization with the façade exactly as it should
be, to conceal the conspiracy within.

Spionage Abwehr was the source of information from which
the Supreme Military Command of the Armed Forces could
reach decisions. It was not the only source; OKW evaluators
solicited and evaluated all kinds of information, but Abwehr
sources and integrity were reliable, and usually superior.
Canaris did not deliver false information. He frequently col-
oured it, as when the plan to invade Spain surfaced: he
unalterably opposed the idea.

His reports to Hitler were presented in a manner to influence
decisions in favour of restraint, but they did not offer views
which might lead to German casualties, nor did they empha-
size anything which would widen the war or prolong it.

Otherwise, while the organization Canaris painstakingly
created was uncannily divided in its purpose, it was also
bizarrely successful in its division, and while Hitler was never
overthrown, which was attributable to factors Admiral Canaris could not control, that goal and the destruction of the Nazi
hierarchy remained his objective even though he knew that
failure more than likely would result. He knew, too, that
national defeat was certain. So did the General Staff, after
1942, when the last opportunity for either armistice or accommodation passed. The difference for these men was that the
Lords of Creation enjoyed the seclusion and privilege of their
Herrenklub where they sat grumbling beneath portraits of
other generals, while Canaris sat in his stuffy little Berlin office
at 76/78 Tirpitzufer overlooking stately columns of chestnuts
and limes in the Tiergarten, perfectly aware that an end to
Germany as he had known it since boyhood was certain unless
his *Landsverrat* – his treason – could bring down Adolf Hitler
and his Nazi hierarchy.

5
Autumn 1939

In accordance with the legend of Teutonic thoroughness, it was expected of German leaders that whatever occurred was the result of competent forethought. A corollary half-truth held that Germans were superior soldiers.

Some validity existed, just enough to ensure repetition of both ideas, but as a matter of historical fact German thoroughness had a way of petering out in a series of noisy obfuscations as at Dorylaeum, Jena, Auerstadt and the five separate declarations of war between 1 August 1914 and 9 March 1916 by a nation never organized to prosecute successfully other than unlimited conflict, while the myth of military superiority hid a concurrent flaw: the German was a good soldier but never a good cause.

Three hours before expiration of the British ultimatum on 3 September 1939 Admiral Canaris and his deputy, Colonel Hans Oster, were strolling in the Tiergarten close by the imposing marble statue of Empress Augusta Viktoria when they met the Spanish military attaché. The Spaniard said, 'Naturally, Germany has calculated this war to the last detail of ultimate victory.'

Canaris's reply was, 'Calculated nothing at all!'

By 1939 Canaris had learned one lesson well: neither he nor anyone else could manipulate the Reichsführer. Also, his hope of support from those stylized colonels and generals of the General Staff had died early. Hitler had successfully used the carrot-and-stick policy, and the *Fahneneid*: he ruled the OKW as surely as he ruled the nation. Canaris's alternative had been to do his recruiting elsewhere, among the associates within his own Intelligence organization, and none of those men had the rank or the contacts materially to abet a successful conspiracy of opposition.

That was indeed a weekend for depression. The half-truths

Canaris and Oster discussed during their stroll had been masked earlier, one month earlier in fact, by Hitler's reply to General Walter Warlimont's remark that no German army had ever gone to war so ill prepared. He would not be such 'an idiot', Hitler said, as to allow himself to 'slide into another World War' (*'in einen Weltkrieg Hineinschlittern'*), like the incompetents of 1914. But at the same time he revealed his scorn both of enemy armies and of such leaders as France's Daladier and 'Umbrella-man' Chamberlain, who were nothing, he said, but *'alte Kaffeetanten'*.

There were not many who believed him. War was coming. One hundred and twenty German divisions ensured it. As Bismarck had said, 'You could do almost anything with bayonets but sit on them.'

That weekend Admiral Canaris spent at his office. There was no way to exaggerate the gravity of conditions. Otherwise he would have been at home at Schlachtensee, the quiet garden suburb of Berlin where the Canarises had bought a modest residence – financed in part by the sale of Frau Erika's valuable old violin.

Abwehr headquarters at 76/78 Tirpitzufer was a maze of dim corridors, creaky staircases, a veritable rabbit warren of little rooms served by an antiquated elevator which groaned and swayed in transit and which occasionally did not function at all. Visitors called the place a 'fox-hole'. It was especially unsuitable for an organization as large as the Abwehr had become by 1939, but the Admiral refused to move or to have the building modernized. Originally it had been two adjacent townhouses, properties of Junkers of an earlier time.

The building had some advantages. It was for example possible to go directly to Wehrmacht Headquarters in the neighbouring Bendlerstrasse without crossing the street. It was also strategically located near the Ministries, the various bureaux of civil administration and the offices of foreign officials.

The Admiral's office was on the top floor, four storeys above the street. It was accessible by way of an ante-room occupied by two secretaries and was a direct antithesis of the suites of other German officials. Outside was a balcony overlooking the Tiergarten and the Landwehrkanal.

It was not a large office. Its furnishings included a pallet for the Admiral's long-haired dachshund, Seppl. There were several filing cabinets, a worn Persian carpet, an old camp bedstead, a desk, several mismatched chairs, an iron safe and two notable wall-hangings – one, the Japanese painting of a grimacing demon, was a present from Japanese Ambassador General Hiroshi, Baron Oshima, the other a large photograph of Generalissimo Francisco Franco, with a lengthy personal dedication.

On the desk was a model of the cruiser *Dresden* and a letter-press in the form of three bronze monkeys, one cupping his ear, intent upon listening, another peering suspiciously around, the third with its hand over its mouth, emblematic of the Secret Services. Above an old sofa was a large map of the world, and nearby hung a picture of Germany's World War I Intelligence notable Colonel Nicolai, of Imperial Germany's Section IIIb, predecessor of the Abwehr.

Aside from the collection of personal mementoes, mostly inappropriate, the office possessed no evidence of power or style. The Admiral was evidently unaware of, or unconcerned with, the impression his office made upon either Party or foreign dignitaries. Several times he refused subordinates' permission to replace the threadbare Persian carpet when they voiced concern at the undignified appearance of the office of the Chief of German Military Intelligence. It was said later that Canaris's preoccupation with the advent of war was such that he probably would not have noticed if the desk had been replaced by a crate.

Here, when Canaris held the daily Kalonne (Column) or staff meeting, his Section Chiefs could enjoy the picture of Seppl on the mantelpiece opposite the Admiral's desk. Here, too, Canaris spent each night of the weekend when war came, either at the scarred old brass-bound desk or at the window opening onto the balcony. With each government office required to display a picture of the Führer, that in the Admiral's office – significantly – showed Hitler boarding the old battleship *Schlesien* and hung behind the desk where Canaris's back was to it.

This was the room he returned to after his stroll with Hans Oster. At ten o'clock his aide, Colonel Jenke, arrived with an intercept: Britain's Foreign Intelligence service, MI6, had sent a coded signal to its stations: 'Halberd', a war-axe for smashing skulls. An hour passed with nothing more. At noon the Admiral set the dials of his wireless set to the BBC frequency in London. Throughout Germany others were doing the same thing. At 12.15 Prime Minister Neville Chamberlain spoke in a tired voice: '. . . This morning the British Ambassador in Berlin handed the German government a final note stating that, unless the British government heard from them by eleven o'clock that they were prepared to withdraw their troops from Poland, a state of war would exist between us. I have now to tell you that no such undertaking has been received, and that consequently this country is at war with Germany . . .'

Canaris told Hans Oster to issue the memorandum which would inform Headquarters Staff, Abwehr, three thousand people in all, that hostilities between Germany, France and Britain now existed.

He then convened a staff meeting and during the course of this conference made two unique statements. National defeat in this latest war, he said, would be disastrous, but victory for Hitler would be a catastrophe. The Abwehr would do nothing to prolong the conflict 'by one day'.

He also made a statement – or gave a warning – to his people concerning their primary adversary in the Intelligence skirmishes which would now intensify, British SIS: '. . . Should you work for them it will probably be brought to my attention, as I think I have penetrated it here and there. They will want to send messages about you in cipher and from time to time we can break a cipher. Your names will appear in files and registers. That is bad . . . It is also my knowledge that they will requite you badly – if it is a matter of money let me tell you, they do not reward services well, and if they have the least suspicions, they will not hesitate to betray you . . .'

As a statement it was interesting, and to a degree quite true. As a warning, it was not required. Both the executive and subordinate auxiliary were absolutely loyal. He had from the beginning treated his personnel with a degree of civility and kindness rare in German officers. At the same time as he demanded unceasing labour and efficiency, he was also accessible and willing to intercede at any time in defence of

Abwehr employees. He was by nature sympathetic and under-standing.

But he needed Abwehr loyalty for other reasons too. War was officially declared at about noon; at roughly six o'clock that same evening Colonel Oster's deputy of Central Section, Major Fabian von Schlabrendorff, appeared at the Hotel Adlon where Britain's diplomatic mission had been assembled for return to London, with a message for the military attaché, Colonel Dennis Daley. Schlabrendorff informed Daley in the presence of Britain's MI6 station chief in Germany, Major Francis Foley, that the opposition to Hitler within Germany would shortly attempt to establish a line of communication with London through the Vatican. He also said that it was Hitler's intention to inaugurate hostilities with a bombing raid on London. In due course this information reached London. Unfortunately, when no bombing raid occurred, British Intelli-gence was inclined to view Schlabrendorff's other statement as another aspect of the *sub rosa* Intelligence conflict which had been in progress between the two secret services prior to the outbreak of war. But in fact it *had* been Hitler's intention to bomb London that Sunday morning. He had been dissuaded by General Alfred Jodl, Chief of Operations Staff (and also by Goering, so it was said later), on the grounds that the British would surely retaliate with a raid on Berlin.

Schlabrendorff's act, as with those who authorized it, was in the Nazi view nothing short of High Treason. Remarkably, neither this episode nor those of a similar nature which were to follow, were betrayed, an incredible condition in Hitler's Germany of authoritarian rule and total police intervention. It was even more extraordinary that this situation existed for so long: until 1944.

For Wilhelm Canaris the formal declaration of hostilities vastly increased his commitments. The secret information which had been reaching Tirpitzufer headquarters for several years from such divergent places as Istanbul and Cairo, Lon-don and Washington, doubled, then tripled. When Czechoslo-vakia was overrun in March 1939, followed in swift sequence by the conquest of Lithuania and the assembly of German might on Poland's border, captured documents arrived daily for Abwehr assessment. On 1 September 1939 at 04.55 hours,

when the conquest of Poland began, Abwehr armed elements
sped ahead to prevent the destruction of more secret files. By 3
September, when Britain declared war, there were crates of
secret documents stacked at headquarters, with interpreters
assigned around the clock. Summaries reached the Admiral's
desk hourly. Synthesized versions were dispatched to OKW
evaluators in a constant stream.

The fall of France vastly increased the load. Confidential information in bales awaited attention from Abwehr specialists.

There was also an accelerated flow of information from
agents in the Americas, Africa, the Near and Far East as dozens
of nations which would either belatedly or never become
participants in the war, reacted.

It was a hectic autumn. Attempts to maintain order at 76/78
Tirpitzufer were overwhelmed by the flood of information. At
the same time, when desperate men in Britain sought through
hastily improvised secret bureaux to organize sabotage and
resistance organizations in conquered Europe which might
divert or delay a German invasion of England, a counter-
espionage conflict ensued which had no equal in the history of
Intelligence operations.

By and large much of this, in detail at any rate, was not the
responsibility of Abwehr Executive Branch. The results,
however, were; details remained the domain of field units and
station chiefs. Executive Branch was rarely concerned with the
names or assignments of field personnel, but critical information and to a large extent the results of special operations were
of immediate interest. Summaries from foreign stations were
expected and received promptly, but which agent or uniformed officer went to bed with which French, Polish or
Czechoslovakian female informant, or double agent, was
commonly screened out of reports which detailed information
secured through such episodes. In cases of questionable au-
thenticity, sources of information were voluntarily supplied;
otherwise the clutter of unnecessary footnotes was avoided.

Admiral Canaris was notorious for his antipathy to lengthy
reports. Many he refused to read, and when station summar-
ists persisted after curt admonitions, Canaris would come
down on them, hard. In a conflict in which the tonnage of
paper probably ran a close second to that of bullets, particular-

ly after Germany's conquest of Europe, no one in Berlin had time for leisurely reading.

But that momentous autumn, synonymous with Churchill's 'twilight war', more than paper and projectiles occupied the time of men in power. What in the years prior to the outbreak of hostilities had been Intelligence skirmishes, now became covert battles. Britain was not alone in the struggle for survival. The German General Staff recognized as early as that autumn of 1939 that the nation's existence was at stake. Between efforts to consolidate battlefield gains and attempts to checkmate politically real or potential enemies at home and abroad, Intelligence operations were increased. Every Military Intelligence network was expanded. Underground counter-espionage throughout occupied Europe was mandated priority until in power it nearly equalled the Wehrmacht.

In London, that autumn, Admiral Sir Hugh Sinclair, renowned chief of British Intelligence, died of cancer. His successor was Deputy Chief Stewart Graham Menzies, Admiral Canaris's World War I adversary in Spain. Originally Menzies' appointment was temporary, but later by royal confirmation he became permanent Chief of MI6. Menzies was confirmed in November, the same month Canaris's tortuous route of secret negotiations was being established at the Vatican.

At roughly the same time, what appeared to be a second line of communication between Berlin and London surfaced in the Netherlands. In all respects it epitomized the covert war. It was also characteristic of the men, and the devious complex duplicity, of the secret war which was henceforth to occupy every waking hour of the men of British SIS, an adjunct of the Foreign Office, and those like Admiral Canaris whose Abwehr Amtsgruppe was an adjunct of the German Military High Command, the OKW. It was called 'The Venlo Incident'.

It seemed to be an independent effort separate from Canaris's attempt to open a channel of communication, but authorized by Germans of equal rank. Menzies of course knew there were many disenchanted German generals: Halder, for example, Beck, von Fritsch, von Leeb, whom Hitler had called an 'incorrigible anti-Nazi,' a goodly score of them, Hammerstein-Equord, von Kleist, even the renowned Gerd von Rundstedt. The idea that Hitler might be overthrown by his own General

Staff had great appeal in London. It was at the same time viewed with scepticism.

The first probes came by way of The Hague, suggesting a secret meeting between British and German Intelligence officers. In the last week of October Menzies sent two MI6 officers, Captain R. Henry Stevens and Captain S. Payne Best, to the Dutch town of Arnhem to meet two representatives of 'the German General Staff'. He warned Stevens and Best to beware a trap and to expect treachery while at the same availing themselves of all options for success.

Steps were then discreetly taken through the Director of Dutch Intelligence, Colonel van der Plassche, to detain the German emissaries while their *bona fides* was authenticated. Even their luggage was searched.

The Dutch Intelligence officer assigned to Stevens and Best, Lieutenant Dirk Klop, gave approval of the Germans, Captain Schaemmel of the Transportation Corps and Captain Hausmann of the Medical Corps. Stevens and Best joined Schaemmel and Hausmann in Best's blue car for the drive to Amsterdam where they were to confer.

Hausmann was Max de Crinis from the University of Berlin's psychology department. Schaemmel was Walter Schellenberg, Chief of the Foreign Intelligence section of the SD. Both were connected with Reinhard Heydrich's subsidiary of Heinrich Himmler's SS. In later years Walter Schellenberg, adamant foe of Wilhelm Canaris, was courted by the Americans. He was also the mastermind behind an aborted scheme to kidnap the Duke of Windsor, but at this time, when he and de Crinis arrived in Amsterdam with Stevens and Best, his purpose was to inaugurate negotiations with the British, not in order to establish another conduit for the furtherance of peace talks but to gain British confidence in an attempt to learn what other conspiracies SIS was a party to against Hitler. The men behind this scheme were Heydrich, Himmler, and Adolf Hitler.

At Amsterdam the German and British officers conferred in the offices of the Continental Trading Corporation, at Niewe Uitleg 15, MI6 headquarters in Holland. The meeting was leisurely and prolonged and resulted in a memorandum to the affect that, 'The political overthrow of Hitler was to be followed immediately by the conclusion of peace with the Western Powers . . .'

When this and related subjects had been agreed upon, Captain Stevens called Menzies by telephone from an adjoining room. Menzies, encouraged but wary, told Stevens he was not to commit himself further until Menzies had spoken to Foreign Secretary Lord Halifax. Stevens returned to the conference room. All four officers then went to dinner.

At dinner the men discussed art and music. Schellenberg recalled later that he was served the finest oysters he had ever eaten. Best suggested the Germans be given a compact wireless set and a code suitable for clandestine communication with London. Schellenberg, complaining of a headache, retired early with aspirin supplied by Captain Best, who then went to an office to take a call from Menzies.

The German proposals were encouraging, said Menzies, but did not correspond with proposals which had reached London from other German sources. Presumably he meant the Vatican. The discrepancies worried British leaders. Best's request that Schaemmel and Hausmann be given a radio transceiver was agreed to. Best then told Menzies that a German general, presumably the principle behind the German plot, was ready to fly to England for additional talks. Menzies agreed to discuss this with the Foreign Secretary, and at that point the conversation ended.

Shortly after breakfast the following morning, 31 October, Captain Best gave Captain Schaemmel a compact wireless set along with a code and a schedule for transmitting to MI6's wireless centre forty or so miles north of London in the Chiltern Hills. Schaemmel's call-letters were to be ON-4. The group then drove back to the border in abominable weather, where Hausmann and Schaemmel crossed into Germany.

About a week later ON-4 signalled MI6 that the German general was prepared to fly to England. The message requested guarantees for the general's safety and for the complete secrecy of the mission, and instructions respecting points of departure and landing. Menzies, who thought the general might be Ludwig Beck, secured approval, then scheduled the flight from Copenhagen on 9 November aboard an RAF Anson courier aeroplane. On 7 November Best, Stevens and Schellenberg-

Schaemmel met again at the Dutch-German border. The Englishmen were in violation of orders from Menzies, who had said there were to be no more such meetings and that if the Germans requested a meeting it should be either at The Hague or in Amsterdam, not at the border.

The itinerary was discussed and agreed upon. The final rendezvous was to take place at the Café Bacchus at Venlo, a Dutch town on the German border.

At this juncture an event occurred in Munich which would have repercussions in distant Venlo.

It was customary to celebrate the Beer Hall *Putsch* of 1923 with an address by Hitler. On 8 November the Reichsführer arrived at the Burgerbraukeller at seven minutes past eight o'clock in the evening to address his Party comrades, those who remembered his first effort to seize power, which ended in a fusillade of police gunfire, flight for Hitler and eventually a jail term.

At twelve minutes past eight Hitler began his address, a bombastic denunciation of England. The beer cellar was crowded. He talked until eight minutes past nine o'clock, was given a thunderous ovation and mingled with the crowd until twenty-two minutes past nine, then he and his escort departed. Eight minutes later a bomb exploded. Six veteran Party members were killed outright and about sixty others were injured.

That same night Walter Schellenberg retired early. Shortly after midnight he was roused by a telephone call from Himmler, who told him of the unsuccessful attempt on Hitler's life. Himmler also said that beyond much doubt 'the British Secret Service' was behind the attempted assassination. He then told Schellenberg: '. . . and this is an order – when you meet the British agents for your discussion tomorrow, you are to arrest them immediately and bring them to Germany.'

News of the bombing travelled swiftly. German newspapers took up the cry that Britain's Intelligence service was responsible. A large reward was offered for information about the individuals who placed the bomb. Hitler's reaction to his brush with injury, possibly death, was predictable. In a rage he called Himmler to give the order for the arrest and abduction of Stevens and Best.

Schellenberg arose – earlier than usual – on the morning of

9 November to meet with his escort of plain-clothes soldiers, commanded by Alfred Naujocks, an SS officer who had been one of the men involved in the clumsy Gleiwitz affair used by Hitler as his pretext to invade Poland. Between them, Schellenberg and Naujocks perfected the plan of abduction, then drove first to Düsseldorf and on to Venlo where Schellenberg went directly to the Café Bacchus. Naujocks and his men remained on the German side of the border, waiting in their cars.

A few minutes past two o'clock in the afternoon, Best, Stevens, Lieutenant Klop and their driver reached the street of the café. At once Naujocks ordered the German cars through the border paling, a burst of gunfire sent the Dutch border guards scurrying for cover, and one German car blocked the vehicle containing Stevens and Best. Naujocks and several companions alighted, ran to the blocked car, pulled out Stevens and Best, handcuffed them, then started pushing them and their driver into the nearest German car as Lieutenant Klop sprang out and drew his sidearm. Naujocks shot and killed Klop. The German car containing the Englishmen then went into reverse and roared backward across the border before turning about to head deeper into Germany at high speed.

By the time the border guards recovered, Klop was dead in the street, the car which had contained Stevens and Best was empty, and the Germans were gone with their captives.

Later, enormously pleased over the *coup*'s success, Hitler received Schellenberg, Naujocks and their companions at the Chancellery and awarded each of them a Knight's Cross.

Stevens and Best were taken to the cellar at 8 Prinzalbrechtstrasse, SS headquarters, and locked into cells.

Among the repercussions of this affair, Menzies's recent appointment as Sinclair's successor came under attack in Britain, and Admiral Canaris's attempt to establish contact with London by way of the Vatican nearly died in conception. The British withdrew from the affair, and except for Stewart Menzies' stubborn perseverance, Canaris's plan might have failed completely. Menzies' contacts in Germany were certain the Abwehr had had nothing to do with the Venlo incident. They were right; no one was more surprised over Schellenberg's *coup* than Admiral Canaris.

6
Days of Intransigence

Germany's conquest of Poland, so swift and complete that even the General Staff was astonished, to some extent minimized the impact of Britain's declaration of war. Thus far each Nazi onslaught had been incredibly successful, and recalcitrants, in or out of uniform, could not denounce success. Not very satisfactorily at any rate. Britain and France had mustered, but sluggishly; there was no talk of peace, but neither was there any very great amount of hostile activity. It was a period of twilight indecisiveness, and an officer of the General Staff said, '*So geht das noch nicht, meine Herren, einen Feind muss man doch haben.*' 'Gentlemen, this simply won't do. After all, someone's got to be our enemy.'

He was referring to the Wehrmacht's willingness to test further its order of battle, but his remark could have been more effectively applied to Intelligence services. Armies know interludes of peace, occasionally as much as twenty years of it. No Intelligence agency rests or ever lacks an enemy, and at this particular time, autumn 1939, the Abwehr had a multiplicity of foes. Many who became actively hostile then, had been only passively so before, and to a considerable extent this was the result of Hitler's Polish design. He curtailed army control and made Poland an SS fief. Atrocities occurred daily. The SS was not responsible to either army regulations or civil law. Admiral Canaris's files on SD and SS excesses bulged. A systematic procedure of annihilation began. There were mass executions of Polish officers, businessmen, clergymen, writers, Jews, artists, anyone who could be categorized as an 'intellectual'. The programme was under the direction of Reinhard Heydrich, a man of absolute amorality.

Canaris's horror grew as authentication reached Tirpitzufer. He flew to an audience with Wilhelm Keitel, Hitler's OKW Chief of Staff and full-fledged sycophant. To the Admiral's protests Keitel replied that these things had to be done; if the army was reluctant, then the SS would do them. As a warning to career generals, when one outraged commander, General Johannes Blaskowitz, protested in person to Hitler, he was relieved of command.

Abwehr files grew as entire Polish towns down to buildings and livestock were destroyed. Canaris's reaction was to make sure that the Generals were informed.

The Generals reacted sluggishly. A few protests were sent to Keitel and his chief operations officer, General Alfred Jodl, both of whom knew better than to bring this situation to Hitler's attention, and while the slaughter and destruction continued, the Generals did no more than they commonly did about things they disapproved of – they grumbled.

But they had reason for viewing Poland in a past-tense context. Hitler was planning now to widen the war in a new direction, and none of the Generals was sympathetic to the old Roman dictum of shortening your spears as you lengthened your frontiers. Hitler intended to launch Operation *Weser-übung* ('Weser Exercise'), the Scandinavian campaign whose primary purpose was to secure for Germany naval bases on the Norwegian coast.

The Navy had since World War I viewed such a move as essential. The excuse was that if Germany did not own those bases the British would. It was also said that critical ore shipments could only be assured through Narvik if the German Navy controlled the coastal sea lanes. There were other reasons, all Navy-oriented, but the Supreme Army Command opposed *Weser* to a man, something which never deterred Hitler, and a special staff (Army High Command XXI) was created for the explicit purpose of making preparations. This staff worked with the Wehrmacht operational command. It was the first instance of the Supreme Command being excluded from preparations for a major campaign.

The Supreme Command shared Admiral Canaris's concern over Poland where the slaughter was continuing, but Poland was to become Operation *Weser*'s first casualty; there was now no time for it.

The OKW, deliberately bypassed by Army High Command XXI, which made a particular point of seeing that the Generals were told nothing, appealed to Canaris, and since Operation *Weser* was primarily a naval operation, the Admiral encountered no opposition in attaching an Abwehr representative, Commander Franz Liedig, to the Special Staff. Liedig, an anti-Nazi, was also a close personal friend of Canaris. He kept Canaris informed and the Admiral did the same with the Generals.

The original plan was to invade only Norway, but there was considerable ambiguity. At several points in early planning even Hitler was doubtful, but Admiral Raeder never was. Nor were the members of the Special Staff. Nevertheless, procrastination continued through February and March, with but one new voice; Reichsmarschall Goering wanted Denmark included in order to provide additional airfields for the Luftwaffe.

At this juncture Abwehr information revealed that the British were also considering landings in Norway (confirmed years later by Winston Churchill).

This information imbued Operation *Weser* with fresh resolve, but the Admiral's purpose in making the revelation had been to discourage rather than encourage the invasion. Britain, he said, had overwhelming naval superiority which could intercept and destroy a German invasion fleet. He felt that Hitler, still wavering, might be influenced to cancel the attack if he were aware of the risks. But in fact Hitler had only very sketchy ideas of naval strategy and listened to Admiral Raeder not the Abwehr. The result was that Operation *Weser* acquired fresh impetus.

There was another result of all this. British Intelligence, which was particularly active in Sweden, knew of German warship and troop-transport build-ups at Stettin and other Baltic ports. SIS had drawn the obvious conclusions. But Admiral Canaris, certainly cognizant of this possibility and faced now with something Operation *Weser* had lacked to this point, an actual date for assembly to begin – 2 April – set in motion his own plans for discouraging Hitler and Raeder.

He sent Commander Liedig to Copenhagen, ostensibly to report at once to Berlin if Liedig found evidence of Hitler's plan being known in Scandinavia. Liedig had no trouble at all; newspapers in several countries including Sweden seemed to consider Operation *Weser* an open secret. The German naval build-up among Baltic ports could scarcely have led to any other conclusion, and every neutral Scandinavian shipmaster who saw it carried the news home with him.

Liedig telephoned Tirpitzufer, reported, then flew back to Berlin, and at a meeting shortly thereafter, Canaris said that now the Abwehr '. . . must do all we can to produce as many alarming reports as possible about British counter-measures'.

Abwehr reports to the Special Staff now stressed the near-certainty of a British fleet appearing in Norwegian waters the moment Operation *Weser* began. But Hitler, whose period of vacillation had ended, ignored Abwehr warnings and gave orders for the campaign to begin, and on 9 April Operation *Weser* was implemented. Although the Norwegians, who had been warned in advance by Swedish Intelligence, inflicted losses on the invaders, no British fleet appeared at this time.

The reasons for this were subsequently explained by London, but they were not very convincing, and in any event the true course of history was unalterable. Denmark fell in one day, Norway held out for twenty-one days, and the best hopes of Admiral Canaris went for naught.

Whether Franz Liedig conveyed a warning to London while he was in Copenhagen or not, someone did, and certainly with the approval of Admiral Canaris.

On 3 April, one day after orders to assemble went out, Hans Oster told his close friend the Dutch assistant military attaché in Berlin, Major Gijsbertus Jacob Sas, that Norway was to be attacked within the week, and one of those exasperating events occurred with which the history of warfare abounds. Sas passed along the warning to a Norwegian Legation official. The Norwegian, for whatever reason, did not pass the warning along to his superiors.

Operation *Weser* was a success, more costly than the Special Staff had anticipated but still a success. Germany had the harbours she coveted, Goering had his airfields, and German arms were now on the border of neutral Sweden. In fact the Swedes were never more than lip-service neutral. They continued to supply the Reich with the means to wage war in the form of ore available to the Germans from no other source, until Allied power made it clear in the war's closing years that a German victory was impossible.

In Berlin the Generals were presented with a *fait accompli*; the fear faded. Hitler had succeeded yet again in the face of all the doom-sayers. There was reason to believe in the future, if not wholeheartedly at least cautiously. Germany had the greatest land force in Europe, vast aerial superiority, and while it had enemies, they could match neither German arms nor industrial capacity. The Generals planned for a regrouping, the creation of a sound hegemony of conquests.

Then Hitler stunned the Generals. In the midst of their cautious optimism, scant weeks after the conquest of Norway, he ordered *Case Yellow*, the lightning-war attack upon Holland, Belgium and France, using the combined might of the Wehrmacht. The only element in abeyance was an inaugural date.

The Generals rose almost to the point of rebellion. With the spectre of Flanders to haunt them, they openly denounced this latest lunacy.

Hitler's response was to order implementation within a framework of months, and Canaris, who had failed to prevent Operation *Weser* and who had accomplished nothing in his attempt to halt the butchery in Poland, saw in the opposition *Case Yellow* generated at General Staff level a fresh, and hopefully more successful, opportunity to influence the Generals. He already had the support of General Beck, who was even more of an 'incorrigible anti-Nazi' than von Leeb, and at least in appearance of Franz Halder, Chief of the General Staff, a conservative and a Catholic, two characteristics which prevented Hitler from favouring him.

After March the element of timing was critical for the Canaris conspirators. Indeed, it clearly limited their options. Once the campaign began, any chance of successfully alienating the Generals would fail. Hitler would drag them along with him.

This time Canaris planned something more substantial than covert attempts at circumvention, although that too was to be tried, and in a form so hazardous that the prospects for failure were great and, if detected, would ensure the execution of the planners.

The near-rebellion among the Generals helped greatly. Men with whom Admiral Canaris had previously had only slight or shadowy contact such as Ewald von Kleist-Schmenzin, Kurt von Hammerstein-Equord, Count Gerhardt von Schwerin, Helmuth, Count von Moltke, great-great-nephew of the field marshal, and others whose rank or connections were invaluable for the Admiral's purpose, were carefully and discreetly cultivated.

An entire host of people came and went as the catastrophe of *Case Yellow* appeared imminent, and as Canaris and his aides concentrated on attempts to circumvent it. In fact in the years to follow the cast of characters achieved bewildering proportions. Names such as Francisco Franco, General Ulrich Liss, Heinz Guderian, the outstanding Panzer commander, 'Baron Ino', the designation of a man unidentified to this day outside Intelligence circles, Erwin Rommel and von Brauchitsch all figured to some degree. Many had only 'walk-on' parts, but it could not be said of any that their involvement was minor. Anyone participating in the plot against Hitler was betting his life, and many such as Rommel lost. There were no casual gamblers in a game with stakes like that.

But the opportunity seemed fortuitous. An attack upon Holland and Belgium, the prelude to total war against France, would compel both passive and reluctant allies of Whitehall to declare themselves. Even the distant and ambivalent Americans would be required to abandon neutrality.

It would lengthen German frontiers to encompass millions of people whose aversion to warfare would evaporate overnight and thereby present German armies of occupation with tasks enough to occupy them without having simultaneously to beat off hordes of fresh foemen.

And yet despite all these clear perils not enough Generals could quite overcome their consciences; there was the *Fahneneid*; there was also a lack of precedent. Never in German history had the Generals rebelled.

The result was hopeless fragmentation. Ambivalence was common. For example von Brauchitsch once listened white-faced to a proposal to save the nation by overthrowing Hitler, did not utter a word of reproach but did not betray the plotters either. This attitude increasingly prevailed. Generals would listen, stiff with outrage, and yet afterwards would not expose the conspirators.

Canaris was to encounter this attitude many times. Or its martial equivalent, an almost childlike innocence, as when General Hammerstein-Equord evolved the plan of inviting Hitler to inspect his troops, then arresting him, an idea so simple in conception, so utterly lacking in understanding. Indeed, when von Schlabrendorff visited the Adlon Hotel as Britain's representatives were preparing to leave Germany on the evening of 3 September, he mentioned this scheme.

Admiral Canaris and his co-conspirators were nowhere nearly that naïve. Any effort at preventing the spread of war at this point required more than simply warning London and arresting Hitler. It would also require an internal *coup* to hamstring the Nazis. To imprison Hitler, whose elite corps, the SS, numbered into the hundreds of thousands, including corps of Waffen SS (Armed SS), would simply ensure a blood-bath with the conspirators as the most likely victims. In a nation totally under arms, force would be essential, but not exclusively so.

There were at this point two Panzer divisions returning from Poland for redeployment. They could be diverted to Berlin. A force that large could handily overwhelm SS guard detachments in the capital. The Nazi clique, Himmler, Goebbels, Goering and Heydrich, could be imprisoned along with Hitler; the functions of government would be paralysed, within hours a regency would be established under Ludwig Beck, a cease-fire would be ordered and, providing each element of the scheme dovetailed, between breakfast and dinner the war would end, Germany would be free of Nazi tyranny and, despite the certainty of crippling indemnities, the nation would survive.

Beyond the establishment of a regency, an end to the fighting and the imprisonment of the Nazi leadership, the plotters had vague notions of inviting a Hohenzollern to return as Emperor. But these things were for the future. Nor was there unanimity about them. The paramount issue was a co-ordinated internal-external sequence of events to ensure swift and orderly transition at home, and understanding, with encouragement, abroad, especially in London. Canaris believed the British would be favourable. He also had reason to expect the German Generals to accede, if not out of desire then out of desperation.

Above all, there was the matter of prompt action. Hitler had equivocated over Norway but there could be no doubt about his determination to inaugurate *Case Yellow*.

In the matter of priorities the Generals would be most likely to co-operate if they had assurance in advance that Germany's enemies were on record as agreeing first to a cease-fire, then an armistice. Canaris, as chief conspirator, had the burden of co-ordinating events. He detailed Hans Oster to establish clandestine contact with London, and Oster, an individual who balanced on the edge of the abyss for years, a man of iron nerve and extraordinary capability, abhorred delay. Nor did he procrastinate now, in 'an atmosphere where high treason and espionage were no longer distinguishable' from each other.

He met with a Munich lawyer, Dr Josef Mueller, who had Vatican contacts. Mueller, a strong Catholic, was held in esteem by Pope Pius XII. Mueller had other friends in Rome, Father Robert Lieber, Vatican archivist, and Monsignor Ludwig Kaas, Keeper of the Fabric at St Peter's.

For Mueller, known to the Gestapo, an anti-Nazi of years' standing, the risks were considerable. Rome was a cauldron of intrigue, espionage and duplicity. What Oster asked was for Mueller to use his Vatican contacts for the purpose of establishing a line of communication with London to inform Britain of *Case Yellow* and request comments respecting terms for Germany if Hitler were deposed and a new government established in Berlin.

Josef Mueller agreed to become Oster's envoy, the two men shook hands, and two weeks later Mueller met secretly with Father Kaas outside the Quo Vadis Chapel near the Appian Way.

In the second week of October 1939 Canaris and Oster learned from Dr Mueller that His Holiness had agreed to serve as intermediary between the conspirators in Berlin and the British, through Sir D'Arcy Osborne, Britain's ambassador to the Holy See. Specifically, Pius would request assurances that neither London nor Paris would sanction attacks or otherwise

take advantage of conditions within Germany during the
course of internal disturbances leading to the overthrow of the
National Socialist government and the removal of Adolf Hitler
as German leader.

The Pope, it was said, '. . . holds an honourable peace to be
possible . . . [and] . . . personally guarantees that Germany will
not be swindled as in the Forest of Compiegne . . .'

In the last week of October Dr Mueller was invited to a
meeting with Father Leiber, after dark, at the Pontifical University of the Gregorians. There, at a conference which was
assumed to be secret, Father Lieber told Mueller His Holiness
had been informed by Sir D'Arcy Osborne that the British
Foreign Secretary, Lord Halifax, had agreed to consider whatever proposals the German conspirators wished to convey.

Dr Mueller, who in any case was not a stranger at the
Vatican, who had now been there intermittently for some
weeks and whose legal prowess and political convictions were
also fairly well known, had been observed with discreet interest by a number of people since shortly after his arrival. The
Vatican, like Basle, Madrid and Lisbon, had spy networks
from all the European powers. The Abwehr maintained offices
there, even billeted its agents exclusively at a hotel on the Via
Veneto, the Albergo Flora. The Gestapo was also there.
Priests, laymen, monks, acolytes, servants and high dignitaries
served as agents and informants. A particular spy was a
Benedictine monk, Hermann Keller, at one time serving simultaneously as an Abwehr and SD agent. Keller had reason to
recognize Dr Josef Mueller. At one time the lawyer had
exposed Keller for making false accusations against a Benedictine abbot. Keller reported the presence of Mueller to the SD in
Berlin. Heydrich, whose suspicions were never far below the
surface, directed Keller to investigate.

During the course of Keller's enquiries he met a lawyer from
Berlin named Dr Hans Etscheit. They spent a convivial evening
together talking and drinking wine. Etscheit was an Abwehr
agent. During the course of their long, engaging evening. Hans
Etscheit told the monk (attired in the robe of his Order and
therefore presumably removed from secular concerns) that
there was a plot in Germany to overthrow Hitler.

In itself this would not have caused great consternation.

Plots against the Reichsführer were not new – before the war ended no fewer than seven attempts would have been made against his life – but Dr Etscheit went further: he named Josef Mueller as representative of the conspirators at the Vatican.

Keller at once visited an acquaintance, Father Augustin Maier, seeking confirmation of Mueller's role as an agent between the Vatican and some unnamed conspirators. Father Maier said he knew nothing, then hastened to the Albergo Flora where Mueller was staying. Mueller immediately left for Berlin.

Keller then quoted Etscheit in a report to the SD. In due course a copy of this report was sent to Abwehr headquarters. At this time Keller's information was limited. He had no idea Mueller was in fact conspiring as a representative of the Abwehr's executive branch.

Oster gave Mueller a copy of the Keller report, after which there was nothing to do but wait, devise adequate cover for Mueller and spy on Keller, who was summoned to Berlin by Heydrich.

At SD headquarters Keller elaborated on his report, stating that Mueller, the German Catholic, was involved in a plot by Jesuits against Hitler. Keller then also saw Hans Oster to say that Heydrich regarded Dr Mueller as part of the conspiracy against the Third Reich.

Oster, his principal assistant of Central Section, Hans von Dohnanyi, and Admiral Canaris conferred. There was no way to deny Mueller's association with the Abwehr; he had served several times in the past, but he could be discredited.

Mueller was summoned to dictate a report stating that prior to the outbreak of hostilities he had uncovered a plot among the Generals to overthrow Hitler. One of the plotters had been Werner von Fritsch, who had been killed in Poland. Another was Walther von Reichenau, a particular favourite of Hitler's. Canaris then took this document directly to Hitler, who read it and dismissed it as being ridiculous.

That same day, in the evening, Canaris visited Reinhard Heydrich to relate in simulated chagrin how Hitler had brusquely dismissed him, referring to Mueller's report as 'nonsense'. Mueller was discredited, and Heydrich, whose instincts for survival were excellent, was perfectly willing not to emulate the Admiral's gaffe, and there the affair almost ended.

Keller was relegated to positions where in the future he would be unable to precipitate crises at executive level, and the delicate negotiations through the Vatican entered a phase of cooling enthusiasm until His Holiness would seek personal disengagement.

Successful reactivation appeared impossible. As Germany moved close to the date for launching *Case Yellow*, security and surveillance increased; mail, telephone and wireless eavesdropping – the SD had tapped the Abwehr lines – doubled, and closer scrutiny of travellers, along with tripled border precautions, made clandestine communication between Rome and Berlin nearly impossible.

It even made contact between conspirators within Germany difficult. It also made those contacts hazardous. Heydrich's suspicions of the Abwehr organization, but especially of Wilhelm Canaris, had been aroused earlier, even before the Polish campaign, the result of scraps of conversations relayed to him from Tirpitzufer headquarters.

As for seizing Hitler, that too became a problem. Well aware that there was strong opposition to his policies, the Führer now adopted a policy of changing residences almost daily, no longer adhered to a predictable schedule, surrounded himself with fanatically loyal SS guardsmen, would see only his chosen clique and began the hermit's existence which he would follow for the remainder of his life – six years.

7

Landsverrat

An Abwehr officer who preceded von Lahousen as director of Section II, Major Helmuth Groscurth, liaison conspirator between Admiral Canaris and General Halder, Chief of the German Staff, referred to the conspiracy as the *'Fronde'*, a name derived from the French insurrectionary movement of 1648–52. But the name by which it was to be known to Himmler's Gestapo and Heydrich's SD – *'Schwarze Kapelle'*, 'Black Choir' – would remain as the conspiracy's designation throughout the war and beyond. It was said to have been bestowed by Reinhard Heydrich, whose personal dislike of Major Groscurth went back a number of years and whose professional suspicions of Groscurth derived from a thick file on the major, who was a devout Evangelical Christian, an unyielding anti-Nazi, and was known to have consorted with all the suspected anti-Hitler plotters whose activities were coming increasingly to Heydrich's attention during the winter of 1939–40.

In fact all the conspirators including Admiral Canaris and Josef Mueller – called 'Agent X' – were balancing upon the sword's edge. Heydrich was a great collector of information. As Security Services Director, he was the Reich's foremost policeman. His goal was control of all police and Intelligence operations, but at the turn of the new year, 1940, he was still essentially a policeman. His concern was internal security. Tirelessly, he compiled files on everyone, even Goering, Goebbels and Canaris, even his superior, Heinrich Himmler – everyone likely to oppose his personal ambition. At heart Heydrich was a manipulator, a blackmailer.

Unlike Himmler, who was an even greater collector of dossiers, Heydrich could not be diverted from a plot to destroy someone. He was deliberate, calculating, absolutely merciless. He would literally lie in wait. In a reptilian manner he would quietly and patiently ensnare his victims. Where Reinhard Heydrich was completely and calculatingly deadly, Heinrich Himmler was impersonally so. He (Himmler) could be diverted from massacre by questions of racial purity, runes, Teutonic myth and fantasy. He conceived secret rituals of German knighthood complete with dark-night sabats in old castles during which naked swords, skulls and hocus-pocus mysticism were part of the theatricality.

He had a dossier on Heydrich to prove that the exemplary Aryan SD chief was part Jewish. Heydrich had a dossier on Himmler to prove that the latter had once associated with Hitler's enemies, and they both had a lurid file about the Führer's syphilis.

These were deadly men, but Heydrich, whom Hitler once classified as brilliant but dangerous, was certainly the more deadly of the two, and it was Heydrich whose attention had been attracted to the Vatican. He began a systematic investigation, employing all the secret techniques available, including the Forschungsamt, or 'Investigative Office', which had originally been founded by Hermann Goering in 1933 to censor mail, tap telephone and telegraph lines and decipher messages passed between police agencies in code.

Heydrich did not require an excuse for his investigation, but he had one. In fact he had two: someone had certainly encouraged the Pope to attempt mediation, and just as certainly someone had revealed details of *Case Yellow*. One was outright treason, and the other one could very well also be.

In the second week of January 1940 His Holiness informed Sir D'Arcy Osborne there would be a German offensive against the Netherlands by mid-February and that the German Generals would move to stop it if they were assured Britain and France would agree to their requirements for peace.

Sir D'Arcy relayed Foreign Office sentiments, which were simply that, although Whitehall felt a revolt from the top could succeed, it very much doubted whether German Generals would have the courage to rebel. Also, while an invasion was not impossible, it was not probable; the Germans were constantly employing chimeras, and this was another one.

Less than a month later Sir D'Arcy again met Pius. This time the German request for absolute guarantees elicited a British response set forth in protocol form: Poland was to be completely restored, Germany was to be 'decentralized', Czech and Slovak territories would be re-established as they had been, the Sudetenland would remain part of Germany, and Austria could decide its sovereign future by plebiscite. Along with mention of indemnities, there were to also be guarantees for the future peace of Europe.

Pius enumerated these terms as they had been given to him, and Father Robert Lieber made the transcription, which was then handed to Josef Mueller, who went at once to Berlin with what amounted to a proposal for the basis of a treaty, which was what the conspirators had asked for. It was called the 'X Report' for Josef Mueller – Agent X.

Admiral Canaris and General Halder met at Zossen to review the proposals, after they had been rephrased in proper German terminology by Josef Mueller, the lawyer, and Hans Oster's principal subordinate of Abwehr Central Section, Hans von Dohnanyi, also a lawyer.

At Zossen it was agreed that Halder would present the proposals to von Fritsch's successor as Army Commander-in-Chief, General Walther von Brauchitsch. When this was done, Halder left the proposals over-night, and the following morning the Commander-in-Chief said to the Chief of the General Staff: 'You should not have showed me this. What we have here is pure treason. That does not come into question for us under any circumstances ... Moreover ... the removal of Hitler would be useless.'

Regardless of Brauchitsch's personal conscience, the nation was at war. He clearly saw no way simultaneously to fight and to argue about fighting's morality.

He had never believed Germany was capable of enduring a lengthy war of magnitude, but Halder's proposal for salvaging the situation was infamous. His final word to Franz Halder was that the X Report should be turned over to the SD, and the individual responsible for bringing it to Berlin should be apprehended.

Halder, already suffering agonies of conscience as he planned the implementation of *Case Yellow* and at the same time schemed against it, told von Brauchitsch that if anyone was to be accused, he was the logical person.

It was an extremely difficult and painful meeting. General von Brauchitsch had little more to say. General Halder, having hoped for collaboration and having got instead an oblique remonstrance concerning the proper deportment of a German General Officer, began from this moment to withdraw from the conspiracy, his evangelist's soul, in the body of a man whose family had given Germany good soldiers for three hundred years, unable to recover from the collapse of what he viewed as the nation's sole hope of escaping ruin. A little more than two years later, in the summer of 1942 at Vinnitsa, Franz Halder's carping pessimism brought Hitler around, white-faced. 'Half my nervous exhaustion is due to you!' he shouted; he stripped Halder of his position as OKW Chief of Staff, dismissed him from the Army and later told Himmler to take care of 'that Bavarian'. Himmler obeyed: Halder was sent as a common criminal to the pleasant, quaint old Polish town north of Munich called Dachau.

Two months had passed; a third month came and went. Originally it had been said that Hitler's latest lightning attack would occur during the winter solstice when no one would expect an attack, but by the first week of April, when Sir D'Arcy Osborne again visited His Holiness, no attack had occurred. SIS's suspicions that the whole thing was another German ruse seemed confirmed.

Pius told Sir D'Arcy he had had no word from Germany about acceptance of Whitehall's proposals. But at this very moment Josef Mueller was again on his way to Rome, not, however, to discuss the proposals but to deliver information from the directory of the Schwarze Kapelle – Canaris and Ludwig Beck – concerning an imminent invasion of the Low Countries and France, along with the directory's denunciation of the attack.

Mueller conveyed the warning to Father Lieber, then visited a Belgian Abbot General, Hubert Noots. Mueller and Noots had two meetings. After the last one Mueller departed for Berlin. The date was 4 May.

Father Lieber told the Pope, who surely passed the warning along to Sir D'Arcy, through whom it reached London. Father Lieber also told an associate, a Jesuit named Theodor Monnens. This priest warned the Belgian Minister, whose response was an indignant denial that such a thing was possible. The Germans, he said, would not do anything so insane.

Several days later Abbot General Noots, a Belgian by birth, also visited the Belgian Minister, Adrien Nieuwenhuys, and this time the warning was more nearly an alarm. The Germans would strike within days, employing the full power of land and air forces.

Nieuwenhuys telegraphed Brussels. On 3 May 1940 the Belgian Foreign Office telegraphed back requesting additional information.

To this point nearly all contact had been either personal, as between Mueller and his friend Father Lieber, or through communications delivered by hand. Now, however, the two telegrams between Brussels and the Belgian Ambassador at the Vatican were intercepted by the Forschungsamt. Heydrich, already interested, received a copy of the Forschungsamt report directly from Himmler along with an order to find the traitor who had warned Germany's enemies. Hitler was informed and flew into a rage.

But Heydrich's Sicherheitsdienst was not invulnerable. Someone passed a discreet warning to Canaris and Hans Oster that Heydrich was following a hot trail. Canaris at once directed Josef Mueller to visit Oster's home. At this meeting Oster told Mueller how close both Mueller and the conspiracy were to disaster, and sent him to see the Admiral at Tirpitzufer.

Canaris placed a copy of the Forschungsamt report before Mueller. An agitated 'Agent X' had no difficulty comprehending where an SD investigation would lead. Canaris then told the Munich lawyer he was to be sent to Rome to investigate the leak for which he himself was responsible. Canaris, using his tapped telephone line, called the Abwehr station chief in Rome, Colonel Hans Helfrich, to say Mueller would be arriving shortly to search for the traitor who had leaked vital state secrets, and Helfrich was to give Mueller his fullest cooperation.

Mueller departed for Rome. Admiral Canaris went to see Hitler, to deplore the treason and to report that he had dispatched Agent X to investigate. Hitler was pleased.

In Rome, Josef Mueller went at once to see Father Lieber. The Belgian Minister, Mueller said, had to leave Rome immediately; SD investigators were sure to visit him and trace back through Nieuwenhuys to the connection between Hubert Noots and Robert Lieber, hence to Mueller.

The morning following this meeting Father Lieber met Mueller again, with a partial solution. A Belgian priest had just left for the Congo. Nieuwenhuys' telegram to Brussels mentioning a priest as his source of the warning about *Case Yellow* did not specifically name the informant. Father Lieber's idea was to implicate the departed priest, who was no longer within reach of the SD, and Josef Mueller agreed.

Somewhere between Rome and Africa an unsuspecting Jesuit was leaving behind the travails of Europe with no idea he was part of a very hazardous intrigue at the Vatican.

As to how the information reached His Holiness in the first place, an even more machiavellian scheme was concocted. It turned upon a principle common to most truly clever circumventions: someone's dislike of someone else. In this case Reichsführer – SS Heinrich Himmler's detestation of the flamboyant Italian Foreign Minister, Count Galeazzo Ciano, Mussolini's son-in-law, and also German Foreign Minister Joachim von Ribbentrop. Ciano was an obnoxious, intemperate extrovert. Ribbentrop was, according to Ciano, 'vain, frivolous and loquacious'. He was also nettlesome, arrogant and disliked by other leaders of the Nazi hierarchy as well as by Himmler.

Mueller's 'investigation' revealed that Count Ciano had learned of *Case Yellow* from either von Ribbentrop or someone in the German Foreign Minister's confidence. This went into Mueller's report to Berlin. When Himmler saw it, he was perfectly willing to believe the worst of Ciano and Ribbentrop.

The investigation stalled at this point. A priest *en route* to Africa could not be apprehended. An Italian Foreign Minister certainly could not be reproached.

Canaris and the Schwarze Kapelle had again survived. But just barely; Heydrich was convinced the Abwehr had become a dangerous source of treasonable dissent. He would continue to probe, and the Admiral's success, brilliant though it undeniably was, had a casualty. The Vatican dialogues ended. British diplomats and Intelligence directors were more than ever convinced the whole affair had been a ruse.

Hitler, prepared to attack through the Low Countries between 1 May and 7 May, was thrown into a quandary by what
had happened in Rome, and as though in confirmation of the
leak, Holland mobilized on 8 May. Hitler postponed the
invasion to the 10th. Intelligence reported that two army
groups, British and French, under Generals Billotte and Prétélat, were deploying north and south of Sedan in order to march
into Belgium should the Germans strike. There were six
divisions of the British Expeditionary Force in this force. In
total there were four army corps. Events, moving rapidly now,
left the final initiative to Hitler. He had amassed the greatest
tank concentration the world had ever known, covered by one
thousand aircraft, supported by miles-deep units of motorized
infantry. He had unquestioned superiority on the vital sector.
He had also recovered from the shock of learning that he had
been betrayed.

Using as pretext the movement of Billotte and Prétélat.
Hitler ordered the invasion to begin on the 10th. His excuse
was that the British-French force planned to drive through
Belgium in order to attack the Ruhr and cripple Germany. One
hundred and ten German divisions, superbly trained and
equipped, attacked 135 Allied divisions. The German 6th
Army under von Reichenau struck Belgium. The 18th Army,
together with airborne troops under Generals von Kuchler and
Student, invaded Holland. Five days later Holland surren-
dered. Belgium yielded on the eighteenth day. France, where
the most terrible blow was struck in the Ardennes, invaded on
an arc from Sedan to Abbeville, withstood the onslaught
rather longer than Belgium – from 10 May to 22 June 1940.

The day Paris fell, Admiral Canaris prepared to fly to
Madrid. He was in the Spanish capital when the paeans of
triumph were loudest. He told a nephew in Madrid, freshly
married, to make the most of his happiness while 'the sun is
still shining', and returned to Berlin in a mood of depression.

He had been unable to impede *Case Yellow* by more than a
few days, his attempt to recruit General Officers had failed, and
the Führer's latest triumphs had closed all the doors Canaris
had hoped might be open to the Germans who wanted a return
of sanity.

At this point, while Canaris's Europe was dying before his

eyes, a question which had been unasked for several years seemed more relevant than ever in the light of the conspiracy's failure during the period of its greatest opportunities.

The Admiral's courtship of the General Staff may have appeared a proper course, but in fact the Staff did not command any troops. Its function was high strategy. Thousands of German soldiers knew of the General Staff only as an exalted abstraction, and at best, if Canaris had successfully suborned Halder or other high staff officers, if in fact he could have suborned them all, he still would not have had at his disposal the physical means of overthrowing Hitler, unless he could have induced one of them actually to assassinate Hitler, to whom these grand strategists frequently had access. (As a matter of fact, General Halder did consider this; he took to wearing a sidearm to conferences and had a number of opportunities but in the end could not kill a man in cold blood.)

Canaris knew most of the tactical generals. His chances of recruiting them may have been better. Heinz Guderian was a good example. Like a number of other field commanders, Guderian lived his moments of victory from Poland to the English Channel in the knowledge that Germany was not capable of winning Hitler's war.

It was the tactical officers who could have stopped the Wehrmacht, not the officers of the General Staff, the OKW or the various councils and committees of strategists, and while the pleasures of armchair judgement certainly derive from someone's ability to look back on history and see where errors were committed, it is also true that men of prescience such as Wilhelm Canaris, who were vigorously extant while history was being made, should have understood best of all what was required to succeed.

It was also true that the Germans supported Hitler for whatever personal motives until his subjugation of Poland, then Norway and Denmark, but after that a very real fear existed. Even in the *Feldgrau* ranks there was a sense of disillusionment, of dread. It required no visionary gift to appreciate that Germany's subjugation of Europe had resulted in alienating two-thirds of the world, and no nation in all history had been able to surmount that kind of hostility, and certainly not such a nation as Germany, whose industrial and military limits had been reached by 1940. It was not hypothetical that Hitler's Germany, like Hohenzollern Germany, could field at best no more than 250 divisions; impressive and irresistible to a point, but nowhere nearly enough to sustain a dream of unlimited empire.

The tactical officers, including Gerd von Rundstedt and the 'Nazi General' Walther von Reichenau (Hitler's favourite and eventually a Field Marshal), Walter Warlimont, Erwin Rommel, Karl-Heinrich von Stuelpnagel, or the popular younger officers at field level, a few generals but mostly colonels, were the linchpins. Even had the Schwarze Kapelle successfully manipulated the General Staff, nothing could have been accomplished without support from officers in the field whose orders Stalhelm would obey.

True, this oversight was eventually corrected to some degree, but not until even such optimists as the Abwehr's Admiral Buerkner had the handwriting on the wall clearly in front of them, and by that time conditions arising from comparative orders of battle between the Grand Alliance and its unspectacular and intransigent enemies made it very clear that Germany's defeat was even more certain than the rising sun, and by then it was also too late, not only for the tacticians to revolt against Hitler's meat-grinder strategy, but also for the conspiracy's leaders, most of whom were dead or shortly to be dead.

The Schwarze Kapelle's best chance for success came – and went – between the beginning and the end of the year 1940.

8

Invulnerable England

In February 1939, more than a year before he launched
Lightning War against the Low Countries and France, Hitler
stood before three hundred German generals at the Reichskanzlei and in an address which was a challenge denounced
two of the highest officers, and not a word of recrimination
followed.

Heydrich, Himmler and a number of Party leaders including
the new Field Marshal Herman Goering were absent; they
expected a rebellion. None occurred.

Hitler himself said later he thought the Generals might arise
to a man and arrest him. It did not happen; he then made a
fresh judgement, and this time he was more nearly correct. The
Generals, he said, were either cowards or fools.

At approximately the same time British leaders evinced a
degree of acuity which Admiral Canaris would arrive at only
very grudgingly, and which he seemed never entirely to
embrace.

Permanent Under-Secretary of the Foreign Office Alexander
Cadogan phrased it succinctly. After analysing everything to
come out of Germany respecting opposition to Hitler, he said
that the people '. . . [with] whom we have consulted including
anti-Nazi Germans of sound judgement are agreed that Hitler's orders would be carried out and that no revolt can be
anticipated, at all events during the initial stages of the war'.

This was borne out once the 'twilight war' ended, when
France was beaten and Britain braced for the invasion everyone felt sure would follow – and which in fact was the ultimate
goal towards which *Case Yellow* was intended to lead.

Hitler carried the Generals along with him when he prepared to launch Operation *Sealion*, the invasion of Britain. In
orders for implementation issued on 2 July 1940, and in
greater detail on 16 July, the same week in which he appealed

to 'the reason and common sense in Great Britain' for an end to the war, Hitler handed the Generals an ultimatum, and they succumbed to a man.

But Hitler – and Canaris – had misread the signals. The British did not want the war to end. They had no intention of yielding; not at this point. Their resolve after 1940 was to use every weapon, every ally, all the means available to them to fight.

At the Intelligence level – Britain possessed as many secret organizations as Germany – the objective was to utilize every capability to cripple Germany, undermine German leadership, demoralize the nation and contribute to its defeat in the field. This meant the Schwarze Kapelle would be manipulated, penetrated where possible, betrayed if necessary. There would be no compromise, few agreements and no promises. Dialogue would be encouraged but trust would not exist. Only one warring nation remained as the sword arm of the European alliance; it would yield nothing. It would use every conceivable means to win.

Hitler's appeal to 'reason and common sense' was not even acknowledged, but when the despairing conspirators signalled Whitehall after the fall of France, still trying – desperately now – to achieve a concordat but offering nothing new except a proposal to replace Hitler with Prince Louis Ferdinand of Prussia – a Hohenzollern – the Foreign Office replied favourably even as a high official, Sefton Delmar, felt that a rebellion of the Generals 'whether successful or not . . . would help to hasten Hitler's defeat,' and even though it cost them their lives, no one in Britain would have any regrets.

The British had their reason: Franz Halder, the old conspirator who had contemplated murder, had master-minded the Lightning War; von Leeb, 'the incorrigible anti-Nazi', had held fast in the south, awaiting an opportunity to advance reinforcements; Guderian, who despised Hitler, had looked forward to overrunning France 'with full confidence'; Colonel Kurt Zeitzler, von Kluge's Chief of Staff, later a General and Army Chief of Staff, had connections with the conspirators; and the entire crushing power of Army Group A, including that greatest concentration of tanks ever assembled, which spearheaded the invasion, was under von Kleist, the same

Pomeranian gentleman-farmer who had flown to London two years earlier as secret emissary of the Schwarze Kapelle to warn the British of Hitler's intentions.

For Wilhelm Canaris the fierce onrush of events was devastating. The break-down at the Vatican, the stunning triumph of arms in France, the confusing situation of the conspiracy's relationship with Britain, and now Hitler's order to all departments for increased activity against the British, intensified the Admiral's position of serving alternate causes, the hamstrung conspiracy and German Military Intelligence.

The conspiracy was certainly crippled. Except for Ludwig Beck, haunting the corridors of power as a leper, and Canaris with his loyal coterie within the rickety Tirpitzufer building, the malcontents were with the troops or buried under the same mountains of paper which now inundated the Abwehr.

Demoralized though the Admiral was, he did not despair. However, the Abwehr was not one man. In Spain for example, the Abwehr, under station Chief Wilhelm Leissner, also known as 'Gustav Lenz', employed more than 600 informers, 717 full-time spies and case-officers, and had sub-stations in Morocco, Algeria and Libya. It also had agents in place throughout the Spanish government with the approval of Iberian authorities. Spanish diplomats in London and the United States furnished Leissner with information which was passed along to Tirpitzufer.

There were also large Abwehr complements in Portugal, Switzerland and Turkey, nations whose neutral windows to the West offered an excellent view of Allied activities.

The Abwehr's reams of accumulated raw information were sent to the OKW's analytical collators of Fremde Heere West (FHW), who, under General Ulrich Liss, prepared co-ordinated evaluations – finished Intelligence reports – from all sources including the Abwehr.

General Liss – who would eventually also be tainted with shades of treason – thought that Abwehr information about Britain was the least impressive Admiral Canaris had ever provided; Canaris, the general thought, 'was not doing his job against Britain with conviction'.

But he was doing it. At least the Organization was doing it. Out of a complement of fifteen thousand people, in numbers at least, the conspirators of the Opposition were almost negligible, and the fact that they were of the executive directory hindered but did not inhibit the organization's efficiency; therefore when Hitler's order to plan for Operation *Sealion* arrived, Military Intelligence embarked upon an Intelligence campaign designed to provide the OKW with the information it needed to plan for an invasion and occupation of Britain.

There had been agents in Britain for some time. Almost none were nationals, which was awkward since the least suspicious spies were those born and reared in the lands where they spied.

Nor had the German Intelligence consortium created a really creditable training programme. Until 1939 orders had been to concentrate eastward toward Poland and west toward France, but to pay no particular attention to Britain. This policy and the lack of funding which obtained up to the months immediately preceding the outbreak of war, were largely responsible for the innumerable Intelligence failures which ensued.

Further, the British had quietly created lists of foreigners, even naturalized ones, throughout their isles. Between the Special Branch of Scotland Yard and MI5, whose concern was internal security, when war came, few agents escaped apprehension.

There were of course exceptions; a few were products of the Intelligence operation codenamed *Lobster*, which Field Marshal Wilhelm Keitel ordered Admiral Canaris to inaugurate on 21 June 1940 and which Canaris passed along to his station chief at Hamburg, Captain Herbert Wichmann.

Lobster was to be the major military Intelligence assault against Great Britain. In assigning its supervision to the Hamburg station, Admiral Canaris had chosen the logical base. But the difficulty remained one not of sophisticated technology, which the Germans had, but of a dearth of people skilled enough to infiltrate Britain or competent enough once they got there to be successful spies and saboteurs.

The Hamburg station was one of the largest in Germany. Before the war its responsibilities had been France, the Iberian Peninsula, the Mediterranean periphery and all the Americas as well as North Africa. Although organizational policy within the Abwehr was ordinarily to limit a station's responsibility to its geographical vicinity – the station at Istanbul, for example, covered Greece, the Black Sea community and ports of the south Mediterranean littoral – the Hamburg facility, with world-wide contacts already established, was an ideal clearing-house for all information, including anything coming out of Britain. It was staffed and supervised by expert personnel and was ideally located on the Elbe with access to North Sea traffic; and among all these and other advantages was a particular one: in separate concrete bunkers in an open field well outside Hamburg were twenty radio stations for both agent-communication and general interception. This very sophisticated and impressive electronic installation could be remotely controlled from the distant Sophienstrasse headquarters of Abwehr-Hamburg. It routinely monitored Moscow, Athens and telecommunication trunks world-wide, as well as secret, scrambled conversations between London and Washington, one of which, between the President and Prime Minister, blew the cover of an Allied secret project later in the war with very sanguinary results. Handling transmissions between agents in Britain and their controllers in Hamburg would be routine.

Also, at Ulm, were an additional nineteen sophisticated transceivers in a wooden building atop a hill just outside the city. At this additional installation London radio traffic could be monitored on all frequencies without difficulty.

Canaris's choice, dictated by necessity, was nonetheless a sound one. There were closer facilities: in Paris for instance and in process of construction at Cherbourg on the Channel coast, but Hamburg was the best, and also the largest.

Roughly a month after Keitel's directive to Canaris for the implementation of Operation *Lobster*, on 16 July, Hitler decided, according to War Directive 16, that *Seelöwe – Sealion* – required aerial superiority in order that a landing 'in England may take place', a clear signal that the invasion was now contemplated to occur shortly.

Three days later, on the 19th, Canaris told Erwin von Lahousen that all operations against Britain had to be co-ordinated on 'an emergency basis', and Lahousen's prompt review of infiltration preparations disclosed that Wichmann in

Hamburg already had two agents in training for an airdrop into Britain.

Contrary to post-war statements to the effect that infiltrating Britain was next to impossible because the British controlled the Channel and the sky, it was not difficult to deliver spies into either Ireland or the Hebrides by submarine. It was done many times. As for an aerial umbrella, that was another fallacy. German secret agents were consistently airdropped into Great Britain.

But getting spies in was not the problem. Obtaining either experienced or talented people was and remained the primary obstacle, and the desperate attempt to make up for the years of neglect on, as the Admiral had said, 'an emergency basis' was scarcely conducive to success, especially against a foe who was canny and very experienced in all aspects of Intelligence, but particularly counter-espionage.

Nonetheless, a very clear need existed. The planners of *Sealion* faced a worrisome wasteland. The scraps of information which came out of Britain were painstakingly pieced together and created a mosaic of contradictory nonsense. British counter-measure and deception bureaux had been a year and more at fabricating falsehoods to conceal the actual weakness of their defence capabilities. One German, General Alfred Jodl, Hitler's operations officer, guessed correctly and on 31 July 1940 said that the Wehrmacht 'need to reckon only with a poor British army,' but no one listened to him. What OKW required was hard Intelligence from sound sources, and there was none. Hitler, relying on intuition, disagreed with Jodl. What Germany faced, he said, was a 'defensively prepared and utterly determined enemy.'

Canaris, his private sentiments uppermost, agreed. He told Hitler that 'not even the Dunkirk combatants' were likely to retreat. Britain, he said, had almost forty divisions, with high morale, well equipped and deployed to halt an invasion. Did he know there were scarcely twenty-nine divisions, poorly equipped, dogged but inadequately deployed? Perhaps, but in any case his aversion to *Sealion* made an impression on Hitler's determination.

Still, the need to know existed and Wichmann's two parachutists being trained at Hamburg were to be the first of a series. Originally their purpose was to have been sabotage, something Admiral Canaris had personally never favoured. He held that dynamiting bridges and destroying factories contributed little to winning wars, were excessively costly and diverted manpower. When von Lahousen instructed Captain Wichmann to include espionage training in the curriculum of his trainees, he did so upon orders from the Admiral.

These trainees were Danes, although both had been born in South Jutland which, prior to 1918, had been the German province of North Schleswig. One, Hans Schmidt, was a grey-eyed, quiet, determined, adaptable man, by trade a mechanic and by choice an ardent Nazi. The other Dane, Jorgen Björnson, was tall, gregarious, a good drinker with a predilection for girls, and was by trade an electrician. He too was an ardent Nazi. Both were in their middle twenties. They had been recruited for the Abwehr by a German agent in Denmark before the invasion, had been sent to Hamburg for evaluation, volunteered for the assignment they were now being trained for and, when the training was expanded to include espionage, demonstrated a degree of satisfactory competence. But the course of training was short. Neither man learned much more than how to transmit simple messages in code on the satchel transceivers they were supplied with. They were not provided with adequate cover stories, familiarized with the countryside where they were to be dropped, or briefed on what to expect when they arrived in Britain.

At a Luftwaffe centre near Hamburg they were coached to recognize various kinds of British aircraft, taught how to make elementary weather reports and instructed in the use of parachutes; a crash-course in explosives was also provided. Then the men were given forged identity cards and ration books using their own names. They were to appear as Danish refugees. Their final bit of equipment was supplied by von Lahousen: £400 each, in British currency.

Escorted by Abwehr officers, Schmidt and Björnson were taken to Brussels and introduced to the Luftwaffe pilot who would fly them to England. He showed them several pre-war maps of England. The drop was first planned to be somewhere along the south-eastern shore, where preparations of defence against a German invasion would presumably be in progress. So the cathedral town of Salisbury was decided upon. Schmidt and Björnson were given several maps of the area to study, and final plans for departure were then left to the weather. The pilot wanted clouds and no moon.

At the rooming-house where they were billeted, Jorgen Björnson, chafing at the delay caused by a lack of suitable weather, cultivated the Belgian chambermaid. Schmidt and the Abwehr controllers became upset. Björnson made an appointment to meet the girl. She did not arrive. In fact he never saw her again. Local Abwehr agents intercepted her *en route* to keep the appointment and took her away. She was handed over to her father with instructions that she was to be locked in her room for a fortnight.

On a dark night in mid-August Schmidt and Björnson were abruptly delivered to an airport near Chartres where the amiable Luftwaffe pilot was waiting. They and their impedimenta were bundled aboard a black Heinkel III lacking insignia and armament.

The flight was by way of the Loire Valley, north-west. Across the Channel the pilot came in under the radar screen and raised Salisbury. Schmidt jumped, followed by Björnson. Hitler's first parachutists to arrive in England since the fall of France came down, hard.

The following day Abwehr-Hamburg waited for news. Nothing came through until near midnight, then Agent 3150 – Schmidt – wirelessed that both spies had landed. That was all. At three o'clock Schmidt came through again but indistinguishably, and nothing more was heard until late in the evening when his call-signal was picked up followed by a message. '. . . At point five miles south-west of Salisbury, Björnson's left foot badly injured . . . You must help us.'

Hamburg contacted Tirpitzufer. Canaris and von Lahousen conferred. Their decision was to run test patterns to determine if possible whether the spies had been caught and were transmitting under duress. One query to Schmidt was: 'Have your identity cards been examined?' 3150's annoyed response was: 'How could they have been? We have not met any British yet.' The next query was: 'Have you used your ration cards?' Schmidt's annoyance was obvious this time. 'No, of course not, for the same reason . . . What in God's name is the matter with you!'

Satisfied, the Abwehr, very reluctantly, contacted its best agent in England, a Welshman named Arthur George Owens, code-named 'Johnny'. Neither Canaris nor von Lahousen was pleased about this; it would endanger a valuable agent. On the other hand Schmidt and Björnson represented an investment in time and money, and so far at least they had not been compromised. At the next contact Schmidt was directed to go to Winchester where, at 2.30 p.m. he would see a 'small man in a brown suit and a brown soft hat' in the main vestibule of the railway station. The stranger would be carrying a copy of the *Manchester Guardian*. Schmidt was to address the stranger as 'Doctor Roberts'.

At 2.30 Schmidt was in the gloomy ante-room. There were *two* small men in brown suits with copies of the *Guardian*. Consistently with his luck thus far as a spy, Schmidt approached the wrong man. As he retreated, the second small man, who had been watching, sauntered up. They left the station together. Outside, Arthur Owen handed Schmidt a slip of paper with a Salisbury address written upon it. He instructed Schmidt to go to that address, where they would meet again.

Schmidt found the safe house that evening. Arthur Owen was there with a second man. They discussed what must be done over supper. Owen said he would meet Schmidt the following morning with a car and would take Björnson to a sympathetic doctor.

The following day, after burying their parachutes and other evidence, Schmidt assisted the lame Björnson to a country lane where they met Owen. Björnson was helped into the car, Owen and Björnson drove away, and Schmidt closed this phase of his espionage career by reporting the details of what had occurred to Hamburg. 'Am separating from him,' he radioed, meaning Björnson. 'Will report some time tomorrow.'

Now was to begin for Hans Schmidt, the poorly prepared spy, a career which should have made British Intelligence blush. For Björnson, the faulty free-fall was a disaster. He was apprehended and spent the remainder of the war in an internment camp. He was fortunate; ordinarily the British executed spies. Possibly his total ineptness moved those who captured him to leniency. Neither Schmidt nor Björnson had arrived in Britain trained to succeed. Neither would have succeeded as British spies had they been dropped into Germany as poorly schooled as they had been, and British counter-intelligence was thought by the Germans to be the best.

Hans Schmidt kept moving. He transmitted twice daily to Hamburg, reporting weather conditions, damage from Luft-waffe attacks and the location of troops in the areas he visited. He travelled south to Brighton, mingled at pubs with locally bivouacked soldiers, reported units, positions, and strengths, identified commanders, commented on arms concentrations, moved leisurely through Kent and Sussex with his satchel transceiver, carrying an ordnance survey map in his pocket with airfields circled by red pencil, and was never questioned. During the Battle of Britain he made occasional trips to London and reported on the devastation there.

In the autumn of 1940 von Lahousen, fearful that by now Schmidt's transmissions had been detected by British monitor-ing stations, directed 3150 to go to Wales, contact a Welsh farmer in Abwehr service and discontinue transmissions until he received further instructions.

Inactivity palled. In December Schmidt's call-signal reached Hamburg again. He was in London, short of funds. Canaris and von Lahousen, operating through the Japanese military attaché in Berlin, instructed Schmidt to rendezvous at Shepherd's Bush a few days after Christmas to meet a dark man carrying a copy of *The Times* newspaper, Schmidt made the contact. The courier was Jewish. He passed his newspaper to 3150 and departed. Inside was £1,000 in £5 notes.

Schmidt now resumed his peripatetic spying, but at both Hamburg and Tirpitzufer it seemed inevitable that he would be caught. If it had been known he was still carrying that map in his pocket with the incriminating red circles, the anxiety would have been even greater.

Shortly after the first of the new year he was instructed to seek employment, go underground and cease transmitting for the time being. It was incredible to Canaris and von Lahousen that he had been able to survive this long, more than a year.

In fact British counter-intelligence had monitored some of his transmissions, but without being able to locate the transmitter.

For the remainder of the winter of 1940–41 Hans Schmidt was silent. In the spring of 1941 his call-letters reached Hamburg again. He was working on a farm and was ready to resume spying, but, he reported, he would be unable to report as often hereafter.

From time to time Abwehr requests for specific information went forth. Schmidt never failed, but by this time he had become too valuable to be used indiscriminately. His reports no longer followed schedule. He reported on the concentration of Canadian troops near Southampton prior to the Dieppe attack in 1942. The result was a blood-bath for the Allies.

In 1943 he reported the activity of British troops mounting a simulated across-Channel invasion, and a year later he wirelessed details of the preparations for D-Day. After the Allies returned to the Continent, he correctly reported strengths and positions of United States divisions in Britain. By then Canaris no longer ruled at Tirpitzufer, von Lahousen was serving on the Russian front, Germany was in her death-throes – and 3150 had married and his wife had borne a child. His last report reached Hamburg as the Germans were preparing to abandon the area under pressure from the advancing British 21st Army Group.

3150 and his family settled down in peacetime London, never caught, never compromised. The last Abwehr agent to transmit before Abwehr-Hamburg's electronic centre was overrun and captured.

9

Variations to the Game

Shortly before the arrival in England of Schmidt and Björnson, the Abwehr sent an Austrian named Ernst Weber-Drohl to Eire as liaison contact between German Intelligence and anti-British Irish officials.

Weber-Drohl, a former wrestler and weight-lifter, had visited Ireland years earlier while touring as 'Drohl the World's Strongest Man' and between exhibitions had formed an association with an Irish woman by whom he had two children. He had not contacted the woman in more than a decade.

Shortly after being put ashore by submarine, Weber-Drohl went to see his 'family'. They would have nothing to do with him, and shortly afterwards he was taken into custody by the police.

With his cover gone – he masqueraded as a chiropractor – his wireless set confiscated by the police, unable to contact Berlin and short of funds, Weber-Drohl became a candidate for recruitment by Britain's very secret counter-intelligence organization, the XX Committee, which derived its name from a contemporary interpretation of the Roman numerals XX – the double cross.

Weber-Drohl was given a small fine plus an admonition and was released from custody. While under surveillance he was allowed a number of days to reach the conclusion that not only was his mission a failure, but he was now destitute in a country from which he could not escape. A representative of the XX Committee, which had been created expressly to suborn secret agents, approached the German with a proposal that he change sides, and Weber-Drohl agreed.

From the beginning, the Weber-Drohl odyssey had little chance of success, not entirely because Weber-Drohl lacked the essential requirements for a successful secret negotiator and spy but because his Abwehr tutors either did not know or had failed to warn him that one of the methods employed by the Irish Republican Army for securing operating funds was to sell foreign agents for cash.

Another *Führertreu* German fell victim to this IRA policy. His name was Hermann Goertz, and in his case the entire charade was a sequence of disasters from beginning to end.

Goertz was an ageing Hamburg lawyer serving in von Lahousen's Abwehr Section II, in sabotage and special duties. He had served with distinction in the First World War. His mission in Eire was to solicit support for an idea originating at the Bendlerstrasse, code-named *Kathleen*, calling for a German invasion of Eire, hopefully a peaceful one, which would provide the Wehrmacht with a springboard from which to invade Britain. As if that were not sufficiently fantastic, Goertz was parachuted into Ireland in the uniform of a Luftwaffe captain, complete with Word War I decorations.

That was only the beginning: Goertz did not come down in Eire but in Ulster. His wireless set was destroyed in the landing, and the small spade he was to use in burying his equipment got lost.

He had no idea where he was, his flashlight failed to function, and although he possessed a large amount of Irish and British currency, once he discovered he was not in Eire, he was afraid to buy food for fear of drawing attention to himself. No one had told him the money he carried was a common medium in Ulster.

Goertz struck out overland, avoiding, hamlets and roads. He swam the Boyne and lost his invisible ink there; then, deciding a hiker in Ireland attired as a German Air Force officer was out of character, he shed part of his uniform but kept his World War I medals, 'for sentimental reasons', and continued his walk in the general direction of Dublin. He wore 'high boots, breeches and jumper, with a little beret' on his head.

Eventually reaching Dublin, Goertz sought a man whose name had been given him in Berlin, and he was subsequently lodged at a safe house, exhausted, thin and demoralized.

The ironies continued to pursue him. The safe-house belonged to a double agent serving SIS.

Someone stole his money, and on 22 May 1940 the police

arrived. Goertz escaped and for a time wandered downtown Dublin without money or contacts, conspicuous in his jack-boots and beret.

A large reward was offered, and the IRA responded, for cash. Goertz was taken into custody, and the only Abwehr article still in his possession, a cyanide capsule, completed the saga; Goertz died a suicide on the floor of his jail cell.

Erwin von Lahousen once said that Germans did not make good spies. Like the majority of generalizations this one was disputable, but certainly pushing men up out of the sea, or out of black-painted Heinkels, on an emergency basis, poorly trained, improperly selected and inadequately equipped, lent validation to Lahousen's observation.

Successful German agents such as Hans Schmidt appeared to succeed in spite of their training, not because of it. One of them, Alfred Wahring, a naval officer in the First World War, gave the British a disaster which nearly brought down the government.

As a naturalized British citizen under the name of Albert Oertel, a Swiss, Wahring operated a watch-repair business at Kirkwall in the Orkney Islands, within sight of Scapa Flow. He observed one of Britain's premier warships, the huge *Royal Oak*, enter the protected roadstead without having to wait until the submarine nets were lowered, which meant the ship was vulnerable from the east.

This information was transmitted to Tirpitzufer. Within days the German submarine *U-47*, under Lieutenant Prien, picked its way through off-shore defences in darkness, fired her torpedoes, which struck forward and amidships, and backed clear.

The *Royal Oak* sank so suddenly there was small chance for escape. Rear-Admiral H. E. C. Blasgrove and 785 men perished.

Incidents of successful German espionage in Britain were greater than anyone cared to acknowledge, but few came to public attention as dramatically as the sinking of the *Royal Oak*.

British Intelligence between wars had suffered from the identical lack of support which had hamstrung the Abwehr. Also, when war came, MI5, and to an even greater degree MI6, had responsibilities thrust upon them for which there was no time to prepare.

MI5 had a far greater burden to bear than its German counterparts, the Gestapo and SD. With the collapse of Poland, Scandinavia, Holland and France, Britain became a goal for thousands of refugees from the Continent. It fell to MI5 to keep track of these people and where possible to winnow out the dangerous ones. It was also charged with discreetly overseeing activities among the neutrals, among them the Japanese, Russians, Spaniards, Italians and Swedes, many of whom were not neutral at all, and quite a few of whom had diplomatic immunity.

Oversights occurred and mistakes were common. The German infiltration of Welsh separatist groups was an example. MI5 neglected to expose an efficient, small network of Abwehr spies and *provocateurs* which operated successfully in Wales for several years.

Reports from these agents encouraged Berlin's strategy planners to give serious consideration to an invasion of Wales – code-named *Whale* – which was to be a subsidiary sequence of an Irish invasion called Operation *Green*. Wehrmacht divisions, to be based in Eire with the IRA's support and sanction, would in theory be abetted during the *Sealion* operation by Welsh nationalists across St George's Channel.

In both Eire and Wales the price of collaboration was to be independence, but in fact the German assumption was based more upon presumption than reality. Neither Irish nor Welsh nationalists were likely in great numbers to welcome *any* foreign armed force, nor was the recent past behaviour of German invaders in other lands conducive to a conviction that they would be any different in Ireland and Wales. Contrary to similar assurances elsewhere, not a single promise of autonomy had been kept.

Fortunately for the MI5 oversight, and despite encouraging reports from spies in Eire and Wales, the directors at Tirpitzufer, aside from their policy of discouraging any widening of the war, did not believe that *Kathleen*, *Green* or even *Sealion* had more than a marginal chance of success.

But the Welsh connection provided German Intelligence with an excellent insight into conditions throughout embattled

Britain. Reports detailing the weakness of defences were filed, and here one of the most exasperating aspects of espionage surfaced. At Bendlerstrasse it was not believed that Britain could possibly be that weak. Hitler did not believe it. Neither did the OKW chiefs. Alfred Jodl believed it but lacked the ability to convince others.

The best an Intelligence organization could do was accumulate information and present facts. It could not persuade generals or statesmen they should act. But if German strategists procrastinated, the Luftwaffe's tactical officers scheduled aerial attacks based on information provided by spies in Wales, the best of whom was the Welsh nationalist named Arthur Owens, known to the Abwehr as V-man No. 3054. Owens was the same man who had been sent to the aid of Schmidt and Björnson and who arranged for Björnson to secure medical assistance for the injury he had sustained in his parachute fall near Salisbury. He was considered the most valuable Abwehr agent in Britain.

Owens first volunteered as an Abwehr spy in 1937 while a resident of London's Hampstead district. At that time he visited Germany many times in his legitimate capacity as a salesman of electrical commodities. As a radical Welsh nationalist, he was 'bitterly opposed to everything English'. He was also troubled by chronic family problems – he had a wife and young son – as well as seemingly insoluble financial difficulties which had for years bordered upon insolvency. Which of these factors or to what extent each of them contributed to his willingness to spy for Germany was not as important as the failure of both MI5 and MI6 to expose him. When war came, and during a period when travelling abroad by Britons was under particular scrutiny by the internal security authorities, Arthur Owens came and went with extraordinary ease, carrying with him specifications and diagrams of armour parks, troop bases, armament factories and naval installations. His information resulted in a number of devastating aerial assaults upon seaports and interior defence facilities.

His selling of information was hampered when it eventually became difficult to reach Berlin from Britain as the fighting intensified. Tirpitzufer's answer to this inconvenience was to instruct Owens to visit Portugal, where a contact would be waiting, and although the odds should have been piling up, Owens made not one trip to Lisbon but several, although Lisbon was a notorious espionage clearing-house and anyone visiting there or returning was normally suspect, even without Owens' dissident background.

Spies in Lisbon frequently served as many as three masters simultaneously, Britain, Germany and the Soviet Union. Later they also worked for the Americans and Japanese. Any Briton applying for an exit visa giving his destination as Portugal was liable to interrogation by British security officials. Owens survived a number of these interviews. Most bizarre of all, while Lisbon was crawling with British secret agents and innumerable freelance spies, in many ways the most enterprising, efficient and dangerous of spies, as well as Russian, American, Japanese, German, Spanish, Italian and even French agents, all of whom watched each other with cyclopean singleness of purpose, no feedback reached Whitehall about Arthur Owens for an extraordinary length of time.

On one trip to Portugal Owens arrived with an astonishing variety of highly restricted information including details of a secret airborne radar instrument, plans for a recently perfected bombsight, and maps of secret airfields. His Abwehr contact, Dr Randzau of the Hamburg office, aware of the magnitude of what he was paying for, was also curious about the source. Owens claimed the material had been given him by an acquaintance, another Welshman, who had recently been dismissed from the Royal Air Force on the grounds of 'political unreliability'. Randzau, intrigued by the possibility of exploiting this source further, asked Owens to persuade the former Air Force technical officer to visit Lisbon.

Owens agreed, and eventually the former officer arrived in Portugal, having departed from Britain without much difficulty despite his suspect status, suggesting a similarity between British Intelligence and Simón Bolívar's army – a great sack with a large hole in the bottom.

There was, by this time, a developing tangential episode to all this which was to have the most bizarre affect upon Arthur Owens and German Military Intelligence. It would also cause repercussions in Whitehall, but MI5 as well as MI6 would be the last to know.

Aside from this, however, an SIS officer, never named, who had for some time been identifying Welshmen serving the Abwehr, was closing in on Arthur Owens, but he seems to have kept his own counsel, because MI5 still had not instituted surveillance proceedings.

There was a reason why this British Intelligence officer kept his secret. While performing routinely for SIS, he was also in contact with American Intelligence. But in fact he was a Soviet secret agent, part of a small, skilled network which had penetrated the Welsh-German connection before the Soviet Union was involved in the war, while upon the far side of the Continent, in Germany, another double agent, this time an American who had penetrated the Abwehr at the Tirpitzufer level, and also before his country was involved in the fighting, was in contact with Washington respecting Hitler's secret reason for delaying the invasion of Britain; he was elbow-deep in plans for Operation *Barbarossa*, the attack upon Russia.

There was a tenuous, almost ectoplasmic connection between these two spies, and Arthur Owens had become, without even the Germans realizing it, the least significant actor in a drama of considerable proportions.

Hitler, encouraged by an adviser, Dr Robert Ley, was of the opinion that, if circumstances could be manipulated which would result in the fall of the British government and a call to the prominent and articulate Welsh politician Lloyd George to form a new government, a negotiated peace would be possible.

Dr Ley, founder of the powerful Arbeitsfront (Labour Front), once likened Hitler to Christ. He was an old-line sycophant, the kind of individual Hitler preferred. It was his opinion that Lloyd George, who had often praised Hitler, would be receptive to a suggestion of co-operation in a scheme which would bring him to power. Hitler, facing balky generals who feared above all things another war in which the Germans had to fight on two fronts, needed peace in the West before implementing *Barbarossa*. If he could get it.

Lloyd George, that leonine old gentleman of outspoken dissent and unalterable opinions, had visited Germany during Hitler's ascendency and had come away with paeans of praise.

He also supported Edward VIII during the latter's abdication difficulties. He was at this time bluntly critical of national policy and even in Britain was thought to favour accommodation with Nazi Germany.

What the American spy had obtained was a verbatim account of a conversation in which it was stated that Lloyd George should be contacted with a view toward reaching an agreement through an exchange of ideas leading to secret German efforts to bring down the current government and support Lloyd George's bid to become the next Prime Minister.

He forwarded this information to Washington, where, after some study, it was consigned to the realm of fantasy.

Someone, however, perhaps in Washington but just as likely from the fourth floor at Tirpitzufer, because Canaris had also learned of the scheme and certainly would have opposed it, leaked the information to a secret agent in Morocco. This man was a British agent who was also in contact with United States Intelligence. The assumption was of course that he would inform Whitehall. (In fact, this spy was a member of the Soviet Intelligence Service.) He reported the scheme to London, which in all probability already had the story from Washington. He also beyond a doubt passed the information along to Moscow.

At this point, and seemingly without any relationship to any of this, the former RAF technical officer who had been a source for Arthur Owens arrived in Lisbon – after having narrowly escaped being torpedoed by a German U-boat *en route* – with more secret material.

As before, Dr Randzau was impressed by what he saw: secrets direct from the War Office. There was, however, one puzzling aspect, for while the former RAF man, in his technical capacity, could conceivably have had access to the RAF material he brought to Lisbon, there was also restricted material from Army, Navy and strategy-planning sources.

It was improbable that a junior Air Force officer would be privy to the secrets of the service arms with which he was not connected, or with high-level planning agencies. Unless of course he had contacts in those organizations which would pass information to him, and if this were the case, then the man

Admiral Wilhelm Canaris, Chief of the Abwehr from 1935 until his execution in 1944

General von Blaskowitz,
C-in-C of the German
forces in southern France

Goering, Keitel, Himmler
and Hitler

General Ludwig Beck, one-time
Chief of the General Staff, opposed
Hitler and paid dearly for it

Hans von Dohnanyi, of the
Abwehr Directorate, was shot to
death by the Gestapo

Josef Gabcik

Jan Kubis

Winston Churchill inspects war damage at the Houses of Parliament, May 1941

Sir Neville Henderson and Sir Alexander Cadogan, August 1939

Sir Stewart Menzies, wartime Chief of MI6, a year before his death in 1968. He had many wartime triumphs, but died under a cloud when his protégé, Kim Philby, was uncovered as a Soviet agent

Gero von Schulze Gaevernitz and OSS Chief of Station Allen Dulles (right) in Berne. Gaevernitz was Dulles's assistant in creating an American espionage organization throughout Europe

with whom Dr Randzau was dealing had created his own private espionage network. But another possibility existed: he might himself be part of someone else's network.

Randzau's dilemma prompted him to contact Berlin. He was instructed to persuade the former RAF officer to visit Hamburg. The man was willing and in due course was flown to Germany, where he was introduced to a number of the Abwehr's executive officers. He was established in an excellent hotel, was taken to the finest restaurants and was debriefed by Abwehr technical experts. He went by the name of 'Mr Brown', was pleasant, forthright, of medium height with dark hair and eyes and was about forty years of age. At his hotel, the luxurious Vier Jahreszeiten in Hamburg, he was under constant surveillance, and clearly knew it, for while his movements were not restricted, he acted with the same frank curiosity about the port city as any other tourist might.

Intelligence experts as well as Luftwaffe officers spent hours questioning him. His answers were given without hesitation, and with complete accuracy. One evening at the bar of the Vier Jahreszeiten Dr Randzau's wife noticed and admired a cameo ring 'Mr Brown' wore on his left hand. He removed it and swung back the cameo to reveal a tiny photograph of a very lovely woman.

Dr Randzau's interest in the ring with the secret compartment prompted him to call Abwehr-Hamburg headquarters at Sophienstrasse. Shortly afterwards, when an acquaintance of Randzau's arrived, Frau Randzau excused herself, leaving the three men alone.

The two Germans drank beer, 'Mr Brown' chose whisky and moments later fell asleep. The ring was removed, its picture of the lovely woman was microphotographed, then replaced, and by the time 'Mr Brown' recovered from his nap – which had lasted a little less than two hours – the ring was back in place.

The following morning in the company of another Abwehr-Hamburg official, named Sessler, Dr Randzau examined an enlargement of the photograph. Discernible was a series of minute numbers and letters, apparently a code. This information was passed to Abwehr-Berlin and Randzau was summoned to a meeting with Admiral Canaris at Tirpitzufer.

At this time 'Mr Brown's' code had not been deciphered, but obviously the former RAF officer was more than he seemed.

Admiral Canaris, who knew more about the Soviet Secret Intelligence Service (called the 'Rote Kapelle', or 'Red Orchestra') than the British knew, had strong suspicions about 'Mr Brown'. He asked Randzau if he had given his word that 'Mr Brown' would not be detained in Germany, Randzau replied that he had. Canaris, the man 'endowed with traits not seen in officers since the first half of the nineteenth century', then said that Dr Randzau's word must be kept.

Randzau returned to Hamburg where 'Mr Brown' and his Abwehr hosts kept up the pretence. Brown would continue to supply his new masters with information from Britain. His new employers would contact Brown when he returned to Britain.

Brown had no intention of returning to Britain, and the Germans had no intention of trusting him. They had all the information they were going to get from him. They also wished to see who he might contact after he left Germany, so he was accordingly booked on a flight to neutral Madrid, which was to be the first leg of his return trip to Britain.

Dr Sessler escorted him to Spain. Abwehr-Madrid had a surveillance team waiting. Brown was to change aircraft, and, between the time he left one to board the other, he vanished.

Some days later Abwehr cryptanalysts broke Brown's code. It was the address of a Soviet espionage headquarters in a neutral European country. 'Mr Brown' was a Soviet spy. Obviously he had been part of a secret ring of Soviet agents which had successfully honeycombed Britain's high-level ministries. The information they had collected, and which was given to Brown to be delivered to Randzau through Arthur Owens, in Lisbon, was part of a greater hoard of Britain's secrets which had been collected for transmittal to Moscow.

The British, who had failed to uncover Arthur Owens, had no idea of the extent of Soviet penetration of their ministries, not during those early war years, not throughout the war, nor in fact for an additional forty years, when probably the last of those wartime Soviet spies, Sir Anthony Blunt, aged 72, a Soviet agent since the 1930s, was exposed in late 1979.

Arthur Owens, the Abwehr's valued agent, had been a

cat's-paw. But the information fed him by Soviet Intelligence had been accurate, and valuable to the Germans.

Why this information had been given to him, and why the triple agent in Morocco was informed of the scheme to suborn Lloyd George so he would pass it along to Whitehall, went back to words spoken by Marshal Josef Stalin of the Soviet Union when it was first thought the warring adversaries might conclude a treaty: the British and Germans must be kept at one another's throats. Anything which might provide even a respite must be opposed. Any scheme to bring a new government to power in Britain which might consider an accommodation with Germany was to be circumvented.

If the West fought itself to exhaustion, there would ensue a great and exploitable vacuum.

No political or tactical weapon which might provide one side with an advantage over the other, down to improved bombsights, the location of hidden airfields, the development of sophisticated small radar instruments suitable for mounting in aircraft, was to be kept secret from the adversaries. Soviet policy was to provide both sides with secrets acquired through its spies in the opposing countries.

In 1941 Russia was accumulating land forces near the Dnieper and beyond. German Military Intelligence knew it, and Hitler's Operation *Sealion* very early became a screen for Operation *Barbarossa*.

To this day some historians attribute Hitler's failure to invade Great Britain to his fear of British defences. He had Intelligence reports of the Soviet massing within days of ordering preparation for the invasion of Britain to be implemented.

He was convinced Stalin would attack out of Poland the moment the Wehrmacht was tied down in Britain, attacking Germany from the rear. So he struck first, invading Russia in the early hours of 22 June 1941, and while the attack was timely, it was too late; he had already begun his war in the wrong direction, and nothing could extirpate that. By then, the Soviet policy of keeping Germany and Britain at war was no longer Marshal Stalin's foremost concern; German might was rolling across Russia with incredible success.

By then, too, Arthur Owens, the Abwehr's valued spy, was

no longer able to supply his masters with top secret information from within Britain's ministries. The Soviets were no longer willing to supply it to him.

He was still in Lisbon and asked to be allowed to emigrate to Germany. The request was refused, and passage was arranged for him to return to Britain. At Christmas time the Abwehr sent Owens its final payment, £500, through the Japanese Embassy in London.

He continued to transmit sporadically to Abwehr-Hamburg but he no longer had much to offer. In the spring of 1941 Abwehr-Hamburg received its final message from Owens: 'Help me, my life is in danger.' Receipt of the message was not acknowledged.

10

The Crucible

The validity of von Lahousen's remark about Germans making poor spies was open to question at any time, but it certainly did not apply to counter-espionage. In this area German ability equalled allied efforts and in many instances was superior.

Decentralization certainly helped. Each Abwehr ancillary, functioning independently of Tirpitzufer headquarters in all matters excepting those governed by doctrine and policy, operated outside another popular myth, that of absolute and rigid German discipline.

As that indestructible master of Intelligence, Reinhard Gehlen (who died in 1979), said, 'The old and well-tried military code that "orders have to be obeyed" has little pertinence in the field of Intelligence . . . The agents in particular and their immediate superiors – the last links in the chain, at the extreme periphery of the organization – must often act independently . . . They alone are in a position to judge whether and in what manner an assignment can be accomplished . . . They are often called on to make snap decisions involving a high degree of responsibility and initiative . . . in general, assignments have to be issued in the shape of broad directives.'

It was the 'broad directives' which, even without urging from Tirpitzufer, governed the operations of auxiliary Abwehr organizations, and here, in the areas of counter-espionage, they excelled. Here too they frequently ran afoul of the monolithic RSHA (Reichssicherheitshauptamt), the State Security apparatus of which the Gestapo was Section IV and the SD was Section III, and which to all intents and purposes was Heinrich Himmler's above-the-law and expanding total police organization.

The friction which ensued never abated. While Heydrich schemed against Canaris and the Abwehr in Berlin, with

Himmler's blessing, in the conquered countries as well as the zones of battle, the competition and in-fighting reflected the antagonisms in Berlin. It was responsible for a prevailing hostility between personnel of both organizations which often hampered counter-espionage operations. At operations level Abwehr disapproval of Gestapo sadism was commonly evinced through threats against recalcitrant informers to hand them over to the Gestapo.

RSHA Departments III and IV never acquired the Abwehr's finesse. Throughout the war they behaved as badly as, and much worse than, they had in the Venlo affair: crudely, violently and clumsily. As often as they could, SD and Gestapo chiefs at RSHA headquarters on Prinzalbrechtstrasse in Berlin, or among the hundreds of auxiliary offices in the field, deliberately exposed, and thus destroyed, Abwehr counter-intelligence operations.

The organization of both agencies, RSHA and Abwehr was fundamentally the same. SD and Gestapo offices existing throughout Europe operated as individual bureaux under the policy umbrella of Prinzalbrechtstrasse, although, because neither Himmler nor Reinhard Heydrich – during the early years of the war at any rate – was involved in the diversionary anti-Nazi intrigues which so often held the full attention of the directors at Tirpitzufer, it was common for the RSHA chieftains, particularly Heydrich, to take active personal control of promising enterprises inaugurated by auxiliary offices.

Nevertheless, Abwehr successes were impressive, and even as the ubiquitous beetle-browed neo-necromancer Rudolf Hess was creating his own Intelligence agency, the Verbindungstab, because he mistrusted Himmler's RSHA and was contemptuous of Canaris's Abwehr, British Intelligence, through several secret service bureaux including a new one, Special Operations Executive (SOE) was preparing to penetrate the Hess organization even before it became operative, although it could accomplish nothing against the Abwehr, even though Tirpitzufer had almost certainly been penetrated after the fall of France by the Russians and Americans.

The main reason for this failure, clearly, was because, aside from an inability to return to the Continent so soon after its Intelligence operations were devastated by the unprecedentedly swift and thorough German conquest, the Abwehr's policy of decentralization had assured separate autonomy for each *Ausland* directory, which would have required separate penetrations, something British Intelligence was incapable of accomplishing at that time.

Even had British Intelligence been capable of penetrating Tirpitzufer, it is difficult to see where this would have had any appreciable effect upon the largely autonomous Hamburg, Paris, Brussels, Ankara, The Hague or Antwerp organizations.

As Bickham Sweet-Escott noted in his book about SIS efforts at this time, *Baker Street Irregulars*, 'As for Western Europe . . . we did not possess one single agent between the Balkans and the English Channel.'

Thus, while the hot summer of 1940 wore along, the Abwehr organizations were able to mend a number of fences, relatively safe even from interference from the Gestapo, which was fully occupied searching out, rounding up and entraining thousands of luckless slave labourers for service in German factories.

Also about this time, Operation *Sealion* as an imperative was fading but not defunct. Its supporters had their plans ready for implementation, even as the inter-service squabbles grew heated.

Thirteen Wehrmacht divisions were to spearhead the British invasion, to be followed by twenty-six additional divisions. Landings were to take place between Margate and Hastings, Brighton and Portsmouth, with airborne elements to land further inland so that the invaders would control a line running approximately from Tilbury over Aldershot to Southampton.

Hitler, preoccupied with Operation *Barbarossa*, occasionally stirred himself to make an encouraging pronouncement which, by late summer, he had no intention of fulfilling. *Sealion* had become a cover for the invasion of Russia.

Germany's blue-water logistical experts declared that there was no way the German Navy could transport such a large force, its equipment and supplies, across the Channel, let alone provide adequate gunfire cover for the landings. If the assault were to proceed, it would have to be on a much smaller scale.

The Generals at once protested. Landing piecemeal elements, one exclaimed, would be like putting the troops through a sausage machine, and meanwhile, as the weeks, then

the months, passed, British Intelligence people began to reap-
pear on the Continent, thinly at first and mainly as organizers
and suppliers for sabotage and resistance squads. German
Military Intelligence began to note this fresh presence but it
was negligible, worth mentioning in reports but only as a
footnote, while at the leadership level Reichsmarschall
Goering came out against both sea and land strategists by
announcing that his Luftwaffe could break the back of British
resistance from the air.

On 31 July it was announced that the invasion would take
place no later than 15 September, with Abwehr efforts to be
redoubled in the interim so that by early September British
defences would be pin-pointed.

But in the meantime other events upset the timetables for
both *Sealion* and *Barbarossa*. In fact, the entire German order
of battle was upset, and the Intelligence sector cast into
disarray as well.

Italy, in a unilateral action, undertook an offensive against
Egypt, and Air Marshal Italo Balbo, who was to command,
was shot out of the sky – by his own anti-aircraft guns – an
event which caused consternation and delay. Italy's flounder-
ing made the Germans uneasy. They had no confidence in
Italian prowess, and a defeat in Africa for Mussolini would
open a back door into Europe. They began to envision a
weakening in the West of their own forces in order to bolster
the Italians in Mediterrania.

Alternatives seemed to be an attack upon British Gibraltar,
occupation of which would sever a British lifeline while simultaneously supplying the Italians in Egypt with tanks rather
than troops. Also, it might be possible to destroy the oil
pipeline at Haifa, where petroleum supplies were stockpiled
for Britain, but in any case keeping Wehrmacht strength intact
in Europe.

Any action involving operations in the Mediterranean impinged upon Spanish interests there, particularly if they involved Gibraltar.

But these events were of concern for other reasons too. What
Admiral Canaris, among others, had opposed from the beginning, a widening of the conflict, was now becoming unavoidable. The *Blitzkrieg* principle was feeding upon its own inhe-

rent law of self-extension, and with that now discernible, German anxieties multiplied. Global conflict, like a stone tossed into still water, caused ever-widening ripples, in this case ripples of widening crises, a phenomenon Germany, having reached the limits of its ability, could not handle.

Economically, industrially and militarily, the nation's zenith had been reached. Allies, not only Italy but the ones to be hurriedly coerced in south-eastern Europe, could provide not additional succour but rather additional millstones. The advantages of pushing the borders of Germany's new empire ever farther from home could become nothing but absolute disadvantages.

That was an unusually hot and breathless summer. Rivers shrank, rainfall failed to arrive, wells ran dry, woodlands sucked up underground reserves of fluid which were normally abundant for both forests and farmed fields, and in Spain, which was largely arid even in good years, an unrelenting sun in a flawlessly pale sky cracked miles of hardpan soil, while the gentlemen of Berlin in summer uniform, white tunics and field-grey breeches with the claret stripe of High Command, conferred at staff meetings, and at the Wednesday Club, to agonize over conditions they felt trapped by.

Admiral Canaris, receptive to the subtle change from west toward Britain and east toward Russia, to the south across Iberia toward Gibraltar and beyond, suspected that, as the only German with complete access to Francisco Franco, the Spanish security service, Dirección General de Seguridad, the Foreign Ministry and the armed forces High Command, he would be called upon to act as Hitler's emissary to Madrid. Accordingly he began developing plans of his own, and meanwhile Alfred Jodl, an indefatigable creator of options, offered an up-dated summary of strategy, suggesting that if the German objective was to neutralize Britain until she could be vanquished by conventional methods, then the seizure of Gibraltar was necessary because it would not simply sever Britain's nearest lifeline but also prevent an encirclement of Germany, which the British would certainly attempt the moment they felt strong enough to undertake it. Implicit in this plan was the idea that, if Britain could be made to mark time, could be held at bay, a German strike into Russia would be safe from the danger of an attack from the rear.

Hitler, already over his head in a seawash of his own creating, in which strategy had become an exercise in desperation, retired to Berchtesgaden, where he paced and fulminated, bent by aggravated kyphnosis of the spine, unsettled in mind by a dawning of terrible doubts, and eventually came forth, as he often did, with a compromise which was a fiat.

Britain was not to be held at bay; Gibraltar was to be seized, then terms were to be offered London, while simultaneously French North-west Africa was to be invaded. Britain, deprived of an eastern empire, would agree to an accommodation, which was the alternative to having a weak but recovering Britain in the rear, but foremost was the *Barbarossa* campaign to which Hitler was unalterably committed.

The Generals were appalled. The original idea had been to preserve Wehrmacht strength in central Europe, in fact to reinforce and augment it for the strike against Russia. Now Hitler's plan for the occupation of Gibraltar *and* an invasion of Africa, in support of Mussolini's débâcle between the Mediterranean and the Red Sea, would dissipate German strength on the Continent, which was bad enough, but Hitler's obsession with *Barbarossa* and his insistence that the Russian invasion must proceed, created an impossible situation.

Even without the dissipation of strength required by an African adventure, *Barbarossa* was viewed as a sinecure only by fools. Recent Abwehr reports from within the Soviet Union offered proof that the Russians were shifting large forces from inland to their European borders.

What Hitler proposed, two simultaneous invasions in opposite directions while at the same time policing *Festung Europa*, was utterly fantastic.

Even Hitler's sycophants, Keitel and Jodl, could probably have been expected to react adversely except that political opportunists survived through servility, and General Jodl prepared the logistics according to Hitler's initiative, and emissaries proceeded to the Balkans – Bulgaria, Romania and Hungry – which were essential to a German strike eastward.

Simultaneously a secret delegation from Berlin, headed by the one man who could succeed with the Spaniards, Wilhelm Canaris, was despatched to Madrid. Travelling incognito, they converged upon an Abwehr 'front' organization, the Excelsior Import and Export Company, whose director was Wilhelm Leissner, chief of operations for the Iberian peninsula, Morocco, Libya and Algeria.

Canaris, who had reached a personal opinion respecting the occupation of British Gibraltar, the African campaign and Hitler's clear design of dragging Spain into his war, sent forth reconnaissance agents to study Gibraltar and simultaneously made certain that the Spanish Foreign Minister, Serrano Suñer, Generalissimo Franco's brother-in-law, understood what was impending.

He wrote a report to Berlin based on information from his reconnaissance agents concerning the feasibility of an attack upon Gibraltar. It was a masterpiece of discouragement and included these points: the British had recently reinforced their garrison on the rock; only one road led to Gibraltar, inadequate in width for mass transport of an invading force; the narrow sea-lane between Gibraltar and mainland Spain was mined. Vigilance and prior warning (through the Intelligence network of Juan March, rich now, powerful and a full-fledged British agent) made a surprise assault impossible. Even to approach success the Germans would be required to commit at least eleven regiments of artillery with no less than thirty-two guns ranging in calibre from 210 to 380 millimetres. Aerial attack would be thwarted by Gibraltar's honeycomb of stone tunnels, and paratroops could not be used in a terrain so steep and boulder-strewn. The same objection applied to the use of glider-borne troops.

Finally, because the only reasonable route to Gibraltar was by land, across Spain, the Spanish government would be required to sanction, and even to assist, Operation *Felix*, as the assault had been code-named.

Here, Admiral Canaris took a personal hand. 'Hold Spain out of this game at all costs,' he told Spain's leaders. 'It may seem to you now that our position is the stronger, [but] it is in reality desperate, and we have little hope of winning this war.'

Machiavelli (or the grey eminence Stewart Menzies) would have cherished this scenario. Hitler would bring pressure to bear upon the Spaniards to abandon neutrality and join the Axis. Franco, fearful of being invaded if he declined, was aptly coached. As part of his price for joining the Germans, he was to insist that Hitler supply him with ten fifteen-inch guns. The Germans did not possess such weapons; they could conceivably cast them, but not before the summer was over.

And indeed, with *Sealion*'s men and *matériel* accumulating rust on the north coast of France, and with *Barbarossa* in abeyance because of what had originally been an Italian will-o'-the-wisp, the summer did in fact slip by.

On 23 October 1940 Hitler himself went by train to the foothills of the Pyrenees to meet Franco at Hendaye. He was prepared to browbeat the unsmiling little Galician whose forefathers had refined the art of barter to a science.

Hitler fumed for two hours before Franco appeared, apologetic and imperturbable. The conference lasted nine hours. Hitler enumerated his triumphs: victory on land, at sea and in the air (although at this time Goering's Luftwaffe was foundering badly). He boasted of an invincible Wehrmacht and an unconquerable German nation. He said that Operation *Felix* would succeed, that Spain's cost as a participant would be low, her rewards high, and that as an ally of Germany, Spain would share in the spoils of international conquest.

Franco's response was the result of excellent coaching. If he became a member of the Axis, he would need those fifteen-inch guns. He would also require grain and petroleum which he was presently getting from the Americans, who would stop the flow the moment Spain allied herself with Germany against Britain. There was also the matter of money – even communications, because the Americans owned Spain's telephone system. And there was the loss of British and American markets, currently a valued source of income.

Until these issues could be resolved, Franco could offer no commitment, nor at this point would Spain join in an attack upon Gibraltar.

Hitler returned to Berlin with nothing. Later he was to tell Benito Mussolini that he would rather 'have four teeth pulled than go through that again'.

But Franco's fear that a frustrated Germany might explode across his borders, as it had elsewhere, was only partly alleviated by Canaris's assurance that this would not happen. The invasion of Africa, Canaris knew, required a neutral Spain.

By the end of 1940 and the opening months of 1941 Hitler's power appeared to be confined between the Pyrenees and the English Channel. But the dilemma of the Generals remained acute. In the concept of global war Gibraltar had never been other than a minor issue; a Spanish alliance had been far more important, and here Admiral Canaris had engineered Hitler's foremost diplomatic defeat. Germany at the crossroads had lost her last chance of acquiring a worthwhile ally. The Balkan hegemony of Bulgaria, Romania and Hungary was a sorry substitute.

Sealion was no longer even a palpable sham; *Barbarossa*, its entire schedule now in the hands of Soviet Intelligence, was no longer a secret. Abwehr reports verified that the Russians were increasing their armed build-up, bringing units into Soviet Europe from such divergent places as Tomsk in the north-east and Leningrad in the north-west.

The hope of an accommodation with Britain was dead. Now fully supported by America, the British could only become stronger. They would clearly be a threat to the German rear, once Hitler unleashed *Barbarossa*.

Success in the Soviet Union could scarcely be hoped for without the full use of all German might. The Generals of OKW, the Generalstab, tacticians and strategists at command level, with a few exceptions, visualized the writing on the wall as early as the New Year 1941. An additional invasion – Africa – could provide Germany with only one thing: a corridor down which disaster would approach, step by measured step.

These were the conditions which existed into 1941. *Barbarossa* and the African campaign would become facts. Otherwise, excluding the American involvement, Germany's war would be waged for another four years within the framework of the events outlined above, and during that entire time the Generals knew how it would end.

For Military Intelligence, whose role would widen with the war, a different variety of conflict was dead ahead. By 1941 the British were back on the Continent, supporting underground resistance movements with more than promises. What had been an occasional footnote to reports in 1940, had by mid-1941 become something altogether different, a counter-intelligence war of considerable and expanding magnitude.

11

End of an Adversary

Stalled in the west at the English Channel, blocked at the Pyrenees by an intransigent Francisco Franco, embroiled in Africa and not yet able to implement *Barbarossa*, Hitler's alternatives included a Balkan adventure through force or negotiation.

They also included something less tangible: fantasy, with which he was beginning to feel more comfortable as frustrations multiplied.

A further factor was beginning to assume malignant proportions. That footnote to the Intelligence reports, British-supported, virulent, armed, co-ordinated underground resistance, was appearing throughout the conquered countries, particularly in the Low Countries and France, first as heroic, rash, almost sacrificial undertakings, then as skilful, well-armed, successful attacks by underground networks of trained, funded, knowledgeably led nationalists with organizational structures behind them which gave German Intelligence its first taste of what was to come, now that Britain was back on the Continent.

For the Abwehr this new peril required a re-positioning of *Ausland* personnel who would otherwise have been assigned to the armies poised to strike eastward through the Balkans. It created an identical situation for the Gestapo, whose responsibility this sort of thing actually was.

As the resistance increased behind the armies congregating for the Russian thrust, Tirpitzufer's warnings that British success in this area amounted to the raising of near-armies in the rear, were shunted to the Intelligence and occupying forces. At the OKW level, every eye – and nerve – was attuned eastward, where the Balkans, age-old route of invasion and now an island between irresistible ideological tides, became an easy victim.

Bulgaria capitulated first. Tsar Boris, who had established a Fascist government back in the summer of 1938, welcomed a German alliance and by so doing doomed his neighbours. When the *Feldgrau* legions appeared upon the Bulgarian-Romanian border to the north and the Bulgarian-Yugoslavian border to the west, Hitler's ambassadors in Hungary affected an accommodation which placed Romania between the jaws of a German vice. She also became a Nazi satrap.

Yugoslavia, facing the Adriatic Sea, with its back exposed to Germany's latest allies, two-thirds surrounded by satellites of the Central Powers, faced devastation or capitulation. It was not even a choice between relative evils.

But devastation came anyway, and in a delayed aftermath, when the first concerted attempt to assassinate a leading Nazi succeeded, both Admiral Canaris and the Abwehr were reprieved in their eleventh hour.

The order which brought about this crisis came directly from MI6 chieftain Stewart Menzies. British agents in Yugoslavia were to promote a popular uprising, taking full advantage of the outcry against a German alliance which followed the announcement by Yugoslavian leaders that such a concord had been achieved.

Three days after the signing of the treaty a rebellion broke out, and its initial success was stunning. The palace was seized. Prince Paul was arrested, and an Air Force general officer, Dušan Simović established a popular government. The German minister was spat upon, British flags, from SIS sources, appeared, and on the night of 27 March a great celebration was held. All this happened in one day. It was to be Yugoslavia's most heroic moment before judgement.

When the news reached Berlin, the Führer flew into a towering rage. He ordered merciless retaliation. From Bulgarian and Romanian airfields German aircraft arrived over the rooftops of Belgrade and for three days pounded the city to rubble. By the fourth day seventeen thousand people were dead, many of them buried in the city's ruins.

The dust was still settling when Admiral Canaris arrived and, sickened by the sight, withdrew to the nearby hills until he could enplane for Madrid. It would eventually be revealed that he had warned Yugoslav leaders their capital was to be attacked. They had promptly declared Belgrade an open city. Then the bombers arrived.

Every German Intelligence organization moved into the Balkans, and the highly effective informant system was inaugurated. Suppression followed and executions proliferated, not only throughout Yugoslavia but elsewhere.

Czechoslovakia, which had been overrun earlier, no longer existed as a nation. It became the satrap of Bohemia-Moravia under a German Deputy Reich Protector. The first of these viceroys was Konstantin von Neurath, a career diplomat of considerable prestige. An intelligent, likeable man who at one time had been Germany's Foreign Minister, von Neurath was a lukewarm Nazi.

At the time of his appointment, von Neurath was in poor health. By Nazi standards his administration was inefficient and slack. In Berlin there were rumours he was to be replaced. It was to be this event which would provide Admiral Canaris and the Abwehr with salvation in their eleventh hour.

In September Reinhard Heydrich would replace von Neurath by direct appointment of the Führer. Before that happened, Heydrich's tireless effort to destroy the Abwehr had come upon absolute proof that a high Abwehr officer, someone close to Canaris known only as 'Franta', had been supplying Czech Intelligence, and through it Britain's Secret Intelligence Service, with documents containing the most sensitive information from German Intelligence and OKW files. According to information captured during the German occupation of Czechoslovakia, 'Franta' had been co-operating with Czech Intelligence since 1936. He had supplied the Czechs with Hitler's plans for the invasion of Greece and the Soviet Union, as well as the armed occupation of the Balkans if treaties could not be achieved. He was still, after the conquest of Czechoslovakia, supplying the underground Intelligence network with vital information which was being transmitted to London.

However, despite all that Heydrich knew about this man, he was unable to identify him correctly. It was certain 'Franta' was a high official of Military Intelligence. No one else could have had access to the information he was passing along. He was possibly on Canaris's staff. At the very least he was connected with one of the Abwehr's large outlying facilities in a capacity of complete trust.

Heydrich needed no more to undertake his final campaign against the Abwehr. Even without 'Franta's' identity, he had proof of duplicity in Canaris's organization, and that was enough.

At the same time he inaugurated a merciless campaign against the Czech underground. In early 1941 he moved against the British-supervised resistance organization known as the Central Committee for Internal Resistance (UVOD), whose leadership, known as the 'Three Kings', consisted of two former Czech lieutenant-colonels called Masin and Balaban, and a former captain named Vaclac Moravek. Only Moravek knew the identity of 'Franta'.

Since these resistance leaders were known to have received information from 'Franta', Heydrich's orders were for them to be taken alive, if possible.

Through its informant system of so-called 'V-men (*Vertrauensleute*: trustworthy individuals), the Gestapo was able to locate a wireless centre used by the Central Committee. It was stormed while a Resistance telegrapher was actually in the act of transmitting to London. Colonel Masin was in the room. He drew a pistol and in the gunfight which followed killed three Germans; then, in a desperate attempt to escape, he fell and broke a leg. He was captured, put to extreme torture, was unable to identify 'Franta' and was executed by firing squad.

During the gunfight Captain Moravek, who had also been in the room, escaped by sliding down an aerial antenna forty-five feet to the ground below and lost a finger in the process. He subsequently reached another wireless station, and Whitehall was warned that the Germans knew about the Central Committee's Prague network.

In London the reaction to Heydrich's success was bleak. The Joint Intelligence Committee, which had a file on Heydrich going back a number of years, which included allegations of wholesale murder, authorized the air-drop near Prague of an assassination team known as the 'Anthropoids'.

Meanwhile, the Gestapo had discovered 'Franta's' day-to-day pseudonym: Dr Paul Steinberg. This made it possible for Gestapo investigators to begin the search for someone whose normal business and social transactions had left a trail.

At approximately the same time, while the Gestapo was painstakingly tracking Dr Paul Steinberg, Hitler launched *Barbarossa*, the invasion of Russia.

At dawn on 22 June 1941, 120 German divisions breached Russia's borders from the Baltic to the Black Sea. From East Prussia came the forces of von Leeb, the 16th and 18th Armies, and the 4th Tank Army under Colonel-Generals Busch, von Kuchler and Hoepner.

From Warsaw came the forces of von Bock, the 2nd, 4th and 9th Armies and the 2nd and 3rd Tank Armies commanded by Hoth, Guderian, von Weichs, Strauss and von Kluge.

From Galicia came the southern force under Gerd von Rundstedt. It consisted of the 6th, the 11th and the 17th Armies, with the 1st Tank Army. Commanders were old stalwarts von Kleist, Schobert and von Stulpnagel.

Another force, ordered up from Norway through Finland by the OKW without consulting the General Staff, as well as Finnish and Romanian contingents, projected an invincible line against Soviet defences, and they collapsed.

Barbarossa's initial onslaught cost the Russians 22,000 guns, 14,000 aircraft, 19,000 tanks and 3 million men.

The Abwehr through von Lahousen, contacted two Ukrainian nationalist leaders, Melnyk and Bandera, with a view to creating an uprising in the Russian rear, and with a triumphant Wehrmacht speedily advancing, an organization called 'Special Services Regiment – Brandenburg' was unveiled. Its function was special missions, sabotage and Intelligence work under arms, and while it was said to have had no precedent in the German armed forces, there were noticeable similarities between the Brandenburgers and the Waffen-SS. Also, more than a century earlier, during the American Rebellion, German mercenaries called Jaegers had served with British forces against the colonial Americans as 'special forces'.

The onset of the Russian campaign terminated whatever stagnation had followed the bottling-up of German power between the Channel and the Pyrenees. All activity, even in such backwaters as the Balkans and France, became accelerated, and while the invading columns strove for goals which the General Staff viewed as nightmares, it became more essential than ever that resistance should not be permitted to endanger the German rear. Heydrich, whom Hitler had come to see as an individual 'more ruthless and less concerned with theoretical matters' than Himmler, was given a free hand not only in Bohemia-Moravia but throughout the Balkans.

By this time Heydrich was convinced that the entire directory of Canaris's Abwehr was riddled with traitors, and while his new responsibility as Protector left him less time to pursue an investigation, he nonetheless assigned his best Gestapo investigators to tracking down 'Franta', also known as Dr Paul Steinberg. Meanwhile, in order to remain secure in his new position, and being cognizant of Hitler's worry that it might become necessary to weaken the Russian front by having to send troops to such places as Yugoslavia and Czechoslovakia for police action, Heydrich announced as his policy the extermination of thirty million Slavs and Jews.

He now had personal access to Hitler. His standing in the Nazi hierarchy equalled that of Himmler, Rosenberg, Goebbels and Bormann. It also gave him the power of life and death over every living individual throughout Eastern Europe, and at the beginning of his tenure wholesale executions began.

On 15 December 1941, for example, in the Cathedral Square of Prague, with a light snow falling, he arranged what was to become the outstanding feature of his rule – wholesale murder.

Opposite the Cathedral, on a wooden platform, was positioned a heavy machine-gun with a sandbag behind it for the gunner to kneel upon. To the rear a pavilion had been erected containing five heavy carved chairs. Swastika banners hung in prominent places; an old man whose duty was occasionally to shake them free of snow walked methodically back and forth.

At 11.45 a.m. Obergruppenführer-SS Kurt Schact-Isserlis, a stocky man with a duelling scar from his right eye to the jawbone, alerted the sequestered special guard detail. Moments later Heinrich Himmler, Reinhard Heydrich, Hans Frank, Prague's Nazi chief of police, and Konrad Henlein, chief civil administrator, arrived in two Mercedes cars and were escorted to the pavilion. The fifth man was Schact-Isserlis, who sat slightly to the rear of the more exalted Germans.

At exactly twelve o'clock the column of hostages was marched forth flanked by armed soldiers. The youngest prisoner was seventeen, the eldest was seventy-four. There were one hundred of them, students, clerks, housewives, labourers, storekeepers, grandmothers. They been sentenced to death by a jackboot court for making derogatory statements.

They were properly aligned, each prisoner standing on a yellow disc facing the machine-gun stand and the pavilion. The guards were marched away.

Heydrich gestured for the execution to begin. The gunner knelt and at exactly 12.15 swung his weapon from left to right, then back again. The movement was too rapid, nor did every bullet produce death. People tried to crawl; blood steamed in the cold. Heinrich Himmler fainted and had to be held in his chair by Heydrich and Hans Frank.

The machine-gunner swept his weapon from left to right and back again a second time, more deliberately this time. When the firing stopped, there were no more outcries and no further movement.

A convoy of trucks arrived, the bodies were thrown in and the trucks departed.

This particular mass execution was an exhibition, the setting and scenario by Heydrich, choreography by Hans Frank and Kurt Schact-Isserlis. The clear purpose of a stage-managed mass execution was to terrify – and horrify – those who witnessed it or heard about it. In that respect it was a success, but this variety of killing was uncommon. Nor could Heydrich, now called 'the Butcher of Prague', or other Nazi leaders be spectators at ensuing executions. Nor were the procedures the same. Every week scores of people were shot, in cellars, behind town halls, standing in fields, in their homes and during periods of German gunnery practice.

There were also 'the experiments'. Innovative surgery, bacterial injections and eventually, because gunfire executions were expensive, the testing of chemicals such as Zyklon B to produce mass death at less cost.

It was this unprecedented slaughter which moved the Czech government-in-exile to request their British hosts in London to destroy Reinhard Heydrich, but it was also Moravek's warning that the Germans had uncovered UVOD, Whitehall's espionage-sabotage organization, that brought the Joint Intelligence Committee to its decision to destroy him.

The Committee men may also have been partly motivated by the knowledge that Heydrich was close to identifying their most valuable informant, 'Franta'.

The assassination team consisted of two British-based Czech volunteers, Josef Gabcik and Jan Kubris. Both were given commando and 'special service' training, then they were air-dropped. They arrived in Prague shortly after the arrival of the New Year, 1942. Underground sources hid them. Neither assassin revealed the purpose of their mission. It was assumed by the Resistance that they were to function as spies and saboteurs, as did other air-dropped members of the Resistance who had been trained in Britain.

The seemingly unrelated aspects of divergent circumstances which were in process of coalescing, with Reinhard Heydrich at the centre, began to converge. Heydrich finally knew the identity of 'Franta'. He was Paul Thummel, holder of the Gold Party Badge, a member of the élite Nazi hierarchy and Prague department chief of Military Intelligence for the Balkans, a Saxon aristocrat with contacts at the highest levels of German social and political power.

On Heydrich's order he was taken into custody, but the customary Gestapo methods of physical abuse during interrogation were not employed. He had powerful friends in Berlin. Also, when the news of his arrest reached London, his friends there became particularly concerned. They directed the 'Anthropoids', Gabcik and Kubris, to postpone Heydrich's assassination and instead direct their efforts at liberating Thummel so that he could be brought to Britain.

Unbeknownst to either the 'Anthropoids' or their underground associates, the Gestapo had learned through V-men of the arrival in Czechoslovakia of Kubris and Gabcik. Nothing was done; the Gestapo wanted Moravek more than it wanted what was assumed to be another pair of British-trained saboteurs. Also, it was the German policy to keep adversaries under surveillance in order to compile a list of the people they contacted. In this case it was to be a disastrous mistake.

Vaclac Moravek was directed by SIS to assume leadership of the attempt to rescue Paul Thummel. Meanwhile Thummel was arraigned before a court-martial board. He denied being 'Franta' and explained his association with members of the Central Committee by claiming he had been in the process of penetrating UVOD when he had been arrested. As he was an officer of Military Intelligence, a department chief, an individual of rank and privilege, his story was one which could be either total prevarication or the truth, and credibility would rest upon the reputation and character of the man himself. Fortunately, these considerations were in Thummel's favour. The military court declined to pass judgement and forwarded its file to Heinrich Himmler.

The Reichsführer-SS conferred with Canaris, then accepted Thummel's defence and ordered his release from custody.

Heydrich's reaction was predictable. In the face of the Reichsführer's order he freed Thummel, but, convinced that Thummel was indeed 'Franta', he not only had the Saxon put under surveillance but moved a Gestapo agent into Thummel's residence to share his quarters.

Exactly one month later Paul Thummel was re-arrested, but during the interim Moravek set in motion plans to get him out of Prague. He was to meet another Central Committee member in the park near Prague's Military Academy on the evening of 22 March, the night Thummel was re-arrested.

Moravek had been edging closer to disaster for several months, since the shoot-out at the wireless centre in fact, which had proved how thoroughly UVOD had been penetrated. This meeting at the park was a Gestapo trap made possible by V-men.

Moravek arrived before seven o'clock and took a seat on a park bench. When the other UVOD members arrived, a hidden squad of Gestapo agents abruptly appeared. Moravek sprang up and ran into some bushes. With a pistol in each hand he opened fire.

The man Moravek had met, Stanislau Rehak, was beaten to the ground and handcuffed. Gestapo agents fired into the shrubbery where Moravek was crouching. A bullet severed the main artery in Moravek's leg. He attempted to flee but collapsed from loss of blood. One German approached, shot Moravek in the head, then emptied his weapon into the dead man's back.

The plan to rescue Paul Thummel died with Vaclac Moravek. Kubris and Gabcik went underground, the Central Committee was destroyed, and Paul Thummel was re-arrested, charged with high treason.

In London, with the last of the 'Three Kings' dead and UVOD destroyed through betrayal, orders were sent to the 'Anthropoids' to proceed with their original assignment.

Their target, Reinhard Heydrich, whose headquarters were at Hradčany Castle overlooking Prague, had now accumulated enough evidence to move against the Abwehr. He accordingly invited Admiral Canaris to visit him. This meeting occurred on 21 May 1942 in the castle on the hill. Heydrich accused Canaris of inefficiency, of political unreliability and of being in charge of an organization which either condoned treason or actively supported it. Canaris defended his organization, but with the proof of duplicity before him and knowing well how Heydrich's prestige, particularly with Hitler, had been increasing, he faced the alternatives of either a thorough investigation of the Abwehr which was bound to be harmful, even lethal, or accepting Heydrich's terms, which included the transferring of certain Abwehr prerogatives to the SD.

Specifically, Heydrich wanted counter-intelligence to become an SD responsibility, which Canaris could accept. Heydrich also wanted the right for SD investigators to operate upon military preserves, and of course this would mean Gestapo agents would have authority to investigate and interrogate all Germans in uniform, including those serving the Abwehr. Canaris could not accept this. If he did, not only would demoralization impair the efficiency of his organization, because in effect it would have become subservient to the SD, but diligent Gestapo investigators would inevitably uncover Abwehr secrets, many of which were nothing short of high treason.

At the conclusion of the Hradčany Castle meeting, a division of counter-intelligence responsibilities was agreed upon. Even some overt Intelligence labours were to be taken over by the Sicherheitsdienst, but actual SD penetration of the Abwehr had been avoided. Canaris had no illusions, however. This was Heydrich's initial attack. He would continue to undermine

Canaris and the Abwehr until he could absorb Military Intelligence into the RSHA.

When the Admiral returned to Berlin, he related all that had occurred in Prague, then directed his staff to ignore the Hradčany agreement.

Heydrich had his initial victory, and while it was not all he had hoped for, it was an adequate beginning. He could return to the administration of his Protectorate with satisfaction and direct the Gestapo to exploit its new powers by uncovering additional evidence of Abwehr duplicity.

He may, on one of his frequent trips to Berlin. have confided in Himmler that he had wrung concessions from Admiral Canaris, although it is unlikely; by now Heydrich's power equalled Himmler's, and the former subordinate was in an excellent position to succeed Himmler as Reichsführer over all police and Intelligence operations. But in any case Heydrich travelled often between his villa and Hradčany Castle, or from the castle to the airport, always in his green 3½ litre Mercedes convertible, always by the same route, always driven by his personal chauffeur, Oberscharführer Klein.

Kubris and Gabcik had for two months studied the route, the road-bed, the general geography, which was hilly, and the personal pattern of their peripatetic target.

Heydrich scorned a bodyguard. Unlike other Nazi high officials he rarely used an armed escort even in Prague, where he was without a single friend among the Czechs.

Heydrich was not a coward. Threats of assassination were not rare. He treated them with the same contempt with which he treated admonitions from subordinates. He believed the Czechs were lacking in 'guts [enough] to do anything'.

On 23 May Kubris and Gabcik learned that Heydrich would use the Dresden-Prague road through the suburb of Holesovice on his way to Hradčany Castle early in the morning of 27 May. They had four days to complete arrangements, ample time to recruit several reliable assistants, one of whom was to be a woman, Rela Fafek.

The Dresden-Prague road made a sharp turn at the bottom of the grade where it approached the Troja Bridge. Vehicles were required to slow to a crawl while negotiating this turn.

The morning of the 27th was overcast and unsettled. Gabcik

and Kubris, with concealed machine-guns and grenades, two companions from the Resistance, and Rela Fafek acting as sentinel up the road, were in position near the turn. The woman was to put on a hat when she saw Heydrich's car approaching, providing there was no escort. A sixth person, also from the Resistance, was farther up the hill with a mirror. He was to signal the moment he saw the green Mercedes.

The assassination squad had been in position for an hour before the man with the mirror signalled. Rela Fafek then appeared wearing a hat; Heydrich did not have an escort.

Josef Gabcik took a position facing the sharp turn, machine-gun in position to fire. It had grass caught in the firing mechanism.

Heydrich's driver slammed the car to a halt and arose, drawing a pistol. Heydrich also jumped up. They both fired, hitting Gabcik.

Jan Kubris hurled a grenade which struck the car and exploded. Shrapnel ricocheted to strike Kubris in the face, creating superficial injuries. Heydrich dropped his pistol, got out of the car, walked a few feet and collapsed.

Kubris escaped, along with the Resistance man and Rela Fafek. Heydrich was taken to Bulovka Hospital after a delay of some time before several SS men came along. Klein, the chauffeur, had escaped injury, and although there had been witnesses among Czechs awaiting to board a nearby tram, no one came forward to help until a baker's cart was commandeered and Heydrich was taken away among sacks of flour and tins of cooking oil.

It was initially thought that his wounds were not serious, although an X-ray showed metal and cloth fragments in the stomach, a broken rib and bits of upholstery leather and horsehair around the spleen. Heydrich had good care and seemed to be progressing satisfactorily, then it was found that he had a spreading internal infection, which became blood poisoning, and eight days after being admitted to the hospital Reinhard Heydrich died. It was 4 June 1942.

His body was taken to Hradčany Castle to lie in state, attired in the black and silver ceremonial uniform of the SS. Then it was sent to Berlin by a flag-draped train for a state funeral.

A reward of 10 million Czech crowns (about £125,000 or

US $600,000) was offered for the assassins. Thirteen hundred people were rounded up and executed out of hand in retaliation; ten thousand others were taken into custody, and the village of Lidice, a mining community of red roofs built around an ancient church, which was where Kubris and Gabcik had dropped from the sky, was razed to the ground. The male inhabitants were taken to a field and shot, women and children were taken away in trucks, then every building was destroyed by explosives and fire.

The surviving 'Anthropoid', Jan Kubris, was killed when a member of the Czech Resistance, Karel Curda, claimed the German reward by directing the Gestapo to a Greek Orthodox church on Ressel Street in the old section of Prague where Kubris was hiding in the loft. But Kubris was not alone when the SS arrived. A furious gun battle ensued. Kubris was killed by a grenade early in the fighting. His companions, unable to escape, fought to their last cartridge, then killed one another.

The Abwehr's most dangerous adversary was dead. At the solemn state funeral Admiral Canaris was among those of high position who attended. Also present was Walter Schellenberg, who was an aide to Heydrich, a man whose 'feminine sensibilities' would prevent him from being anything but a genuine mediocrity with a chameleon-like propensity for switching loyalties on a moment's notice. He was thirty-two years old when he attended Heydrich's funeral.

What Heydrich's passing particularly accomplished was a guarantee that the Abwehr would continue to survive as Admiral Canaris's autonomous organization free of RSHA control, but now, in midsummer 1942, with German armies triumphant but lost in space across the endless kilometres of Russia, Hitler's 120 divisions had become a thin grey line, while the 200 Soviet divisions reported by Military Intelligence turned out to be 360 divisions, and those were the ones which had been identified. There were many more, and this kind of mistake could be disastrous. For the first time the heretofore reliable and prestigious Military Intelligence, Abwehr, came up for strong censure even from its friends; from the Führer came accusations of dereliction and, more ominous, unreliability. In Nazi Germany 'unreliability' was synonymous with treason.

12

The Patchwork Rebellion

Hitler's superb war machine rolled up a list of victories in the early months of the Russian campaign which were unequalled. Soviet losses were incredible. Despite the fact that Russian Intelligence knew the attack was coming, where it would occur and how many German divisions were available, when the invasion began and for months afterwards, nothing the Russians could do made any difference, and this amply demonstrated how, under certain circumstances, Intelligence was nearly useless.

To know an enemy was coming, to be able to define his motives and strength down to the last man and the last gun, meant nothing if he had overwhelming superiority in strength, which the Germans certainly possessed during the early stages of their Russian thrust.

Barbarossa was not a conflict of Intelligence services the way the campaigns of central Europe had been. There had never been the kind of wholesale slaughter in Europe that there was in Russia. In comparison Hitler's Continental conquests were almost textbook examples of orthodox warfare.

By midsummer 1942 Russia was a charnel house. At Kiev the previous September nearly a million Russians under Budenny were beaten in a battle of appalling brutality. Six hundred thousand of them were captured, the dead dragged into lines more than a mile long. Nearly one third of the Soviet army, as it had been when the eastern war began, had been captured or killed.

The barbarism was not confined to battlefields. The Russians rounded up and executed thousands of their own people. Both sides shot prisoners. The wounded were allowed to die through deliberate neglect, and the German conquest continued.

It was a campaign scaled to the size of the area where it was being fought. For a long time a vacuum existed; Europeans heard the most improbable rumours but generally did not believe them, and because Europeans were existing in an insular world of their own misery, the events a thousand miles away, between contestants they could not identify with, did not matter. The vacuum could exist, did exist, and in such places as France and the Low Countries could continue to exist.

In Russia the war did not move according to the dictates of politics or even ideologies; it was purely and simply a contest between meat-grinders. It would remain that way throughout the summer and autumn of 1942, an unprecedented example of the absolute worst in human nature.

The Intelligence war was being waged in Europe, its intensity increasing as German preoccupation in the East mitigated what had previously been Germany's primary concern, the occupation and suppression of conquered countries, their exploitation and administration, and the increase in resistance gave German strategists good cause for anxiety, because as the Intelligence war grew, its fundamental reason for existing at all – an Allied invasion of Europe – was discernible. The one element above all others which Germany's professional soldiers feared, a war on two fronts, had to be stalemated at all costs.

Hitler's prediction of an early triumph in Russia, while it seemed possible at first, did not make a dent in the solidly grounded pessimism of the grand strategists in Berlin. Their alternative, once the Führer attacked Russia, was to try to buy him the time for victory – whether it was obtained or not – by securing the coasts of France in particular against the Allied invasion which would bring on the two-front war and ensure Germany's destruction.

Toward this end the Intelligence services throughout occupied Europe were strengthened, and although Himmler's Security Services, the SD and Gestapo, had been constituted for precisely this sort of thing, how important it was thought to be was evinced when Military Intelligence became involved in the struggle against civilian nationalist movements. In Europe during 1942–3 the paramount issue was counter-intelligence.

The subsequent criticism that German counter-intelligence

people were so numerous and had so much overlapping of authority that they literally stumbled over one another was true, but what critics tended to lose sight of was that this very duplication resulted in successes that historians of the war, for whatever reasons, have generally ignored. The best Allied espionage-sabotage efforts were monitored by German Intelligence. The largest secret underground organizations were penetrated, and one particular Allied agency, Special Operations Executive, emerged from the war with a carefully nurtured cover of ingenious success when in fact it had a deplorable record of losing people, of being duped into air-dropping caches of weapons and funds into waiting German hands, and of utilizing some very talented, skilled people in undertakings which had practically no chance of success.

Nor were the rivalries among German Intelligence organizations unique. The British in particular were plagued by this situation. When Special Operations Executive was initially organized, there was considerable dispute over what government department should control it: the Foreign Office, the War Office, SIS, the Ministry of Information or the Ministry of Economic Warfare (a misleading name: MEW dealt in black propaganda, subversive warfare and 'dirty tricks'; it also possessed an excellent Intelligence department).

SOE eventually became a separate department, but the resentment against it from agencies which felt it had trespassed on their turf never entirely abated. As the Gestapo was hostile to the Abwehr, so was SIS resentful of Special Operations Executive. Neither British Military Intelligence nor SIS was pleased at the prospect of a new organization entering their field – SIS because two of its departments, one concerned with industrial sabotage and irregular warfare, the other with political and economic subversion, were detached to become part of SOE; the War Office because it also lost a department to SOE, Military Intelligence Research – MIR. In fact it was an assistant to the chief of MIR, Lieutenant-Colonel Colin Gubbins, who would eventually become the head of SOE.

Originally, SOE was intended to serve the Allied interests in sabotage and subversion. Its agents were recruited and trained for those purposes. But Prime Minister Churchill, whose brainchild SOE was, envisioned a broader scope, as evidenced when in a memorandum to War Secretary Anthony Eden he wrote: 'It is . . . urgent and indispensable that every [SOE] effort should be made to obtain secretly the best possible information about the German forces in the various countries overrun, and to establish intimate contacts with local people, and to plant agents.'

Special Operations Executive, whose purpose and training methods were to export people to engage in sabotage and subversion, was now also to spy.

Britain, like Germany, had more than enough Intelligence organizations. Aside from Military and Naval, Foreign Office and Ministry of Economic Warfare Intelligence bureaux, there were SIS, the XX Committee and several others. Added to the list now was Special Operations Executive. It was not generally welcomed by the others, nor accepted. Nor was its training programme designed to produce spies.

Further, SOE objectives were thought by several governments in exile, such as the French, Dutch and Norwegian, to be incompatible with those governments' interests. The French in particular were antagonistic; General de Gaulle was especially hostile. He claimed that the British supported only those Resistance movements whose policies reflected Britain's political interests. He never stopped accusing the British and Americans of trying to undercut his influence on the Continent, nor did he overlook an opportunity to create antagonism. At least once in an attempt to anticipate Allied plans he called for an uprising in France before the Allies were ready to support it, and the Germans' reaction was brutal suppression with considerable loss of life.

On the Continent too, SOE ran head-on into an additional array of divergent allegiances. Not all Frenchmen were Gaullists. There were left- and right-wing groups, as well as liberal — or conservative — Socialists. There were radicals, separatists and Pétainists (not many), plus splinter groups loyal to individual, local partisan leaders. And there were ambitious Resistance leaders who saw themselves as the saviours of France, and its future leaders. To these men every other potential leader was anathema, and except for sharing a mutual hatred for Germans, they were suspicious of one another and quite willing to play politics.

Finally for SOE there were the Germans. Their counter-intelligence tentacles reached everywhere. They were experienced, and they had developed their V-man system very well. They had also perfected other techniques. Lieutenant-Colonel Herman Giskes, section chief of Abwehr III-F in Holland, revealed how Military Intelligence had been able to neutralize SIS operations in The Hague: through the portholes of a canal barge, Abwehr photographers took pictures from a distance of less than thirty yards of the entire Secret Service staff and 'recorded with complete accuracy the names, cover-names, assigned duties, activities and contacts of every . . . one [of them]'.

Another feature which created difficulties, not just for SOE but for all Allied Intelligence operations, was the British policy of forbidding governments in exile to operate independently. For obvious reasons the British could not permit the French, for example, or the Dutch, Norwegians or others to initiate clandestine operations of which the British knew nothing. Aside from the possibility that their own secret operations might be jeopardized, guest governments in Britain could bring on powerful German reactions in areas where Britain was unprepared to meet them.

But justified or not, in this era of intense national sentiment the exile governments, each with its own Intelligence service, chafed at British control. They particularly disapproved of the British policy that required all exile Intelligence organizations to list agents with the British, to co-ordinate all secret activities and to submit secret agents to British training and direction, and every subsequent Intelligence disaster on the Continent caused an uproar. The responsibility British Intelligence incurred, the moment it assumed direction of exile clandestine activity, ensured accusations of inefficiency at best, and treachery at the worst.

The Dutch government, for example, reluctantly yielded to British requirements that its secret agents sent to the Netherlands be identified first and their purpose approved of. Subsequently they were captured almost to a man, and Dutch officials accused the British of complete culpability, even deliberate treachery.

In fact, the Abwehr had successfully taken over the SOE's

clandestine radio stations. From these sources they got not only the names of agents to be air-dropped in the Netherlands but the dates of arrival. These same 'turned-around' wireless centres fed false information to British Intelligence for a considerable period of time, almost two years.

The Germans, after all, had been perfecting their counter-intelligence techniques on the Continent for several years. In that length of time Abwehr and Gestapo expertise had reached a point where even the most skilled Intelligence people operating out of London faced unnerving odds. People such as those sent in by SOE were sitting ducks.

But others who were in positions which enabled them to know more were equally as negligent.

Charles de Gaulle, who on several occasions flatly refused to co-operate with British Intelligence, conducted a secret war by his own rules.

His Intelligence organization, the Bureau Central de Renseignements et d'Action (BCRA), established contact with Resistance leaders in France, and BCRA's Colonel Passy laboured diligently to create enough harmony among French underground leaders so that an Armée Secrète could be organized. He was successful, and SOE supplied the arms.

In command was General Charles Delestraint (also known as General Vidal). But the Armée Secrète had its own built-in failure-factor, and in retrospect it seems that an epitome of naïveté had to exist for Passy, Delestraint, the French Section of SOE and Charles de Gaulle not to realize, in view of what they knew by 1942–3 of German thoroughness, that large armed groups could not be organized in France without the Germans knowing about them. And this was a large organization.

It was established along regional lines with a command structure to co-ordinate the various, and numerous, sub-commands. SOE liaison officials and armed service instructors were supplied. Arms caches were established, wireless centres set up, a vigorous recruiting campaign undertaken.

Jean Moulin, a former prefect of Chartres, was de Gaulle's personal representative. He was a man of tireless energy and great courage.

De Gaulle's exhilaration was understandable, for his secret

army was growing. It had arms, high morale and adequate leadership. It also had Abwehr and SD V-men on several of its staffs. The Germans knew as much about the Armée Secrète as did de Gaulle. They knew more; they knew how to destroy it. When they were ready, Jean Moulin was arrested and died under torture, General Delestraint was shot, regional leaders were arrested by the score, the organization was fragmented, its survivors driven underground, and only two elements remained, the French will to resist and some of the caches of arms.

For SOE the disaster was a prelude and a lesson. German counter-intelligence was thoroughly entrenched. It was also very capable. The story of how Abwehr agents broke Interallié, the widespread Resistance organization with cells in every sector of German-occupied France has been told elsewhere— see *Mathilde Carré, Double Agent* – but an equally successful *coup* in Holland has received less attention although it was certainly as damaging to Allied aspirations.

In the last week of June 1942 a Dutch agent was sent to Holland to co-ordinate Resistance efforts and to implement *Plan Holland*, a scheme approved by the Allied Chiefs of Staff to organize the Netherlands underground. The agent was George Louis Jambroes, a peace-time educator. With him went his 'pianist', his radio-operator, Joseph Bukkens.

The Abwehr, in control of Netherlands Resistance wireless stations, was waiting. Jambroes and Bukkens were apprehended upon their arrival, and Bukkens' radio was 'turned around'. For six months the Abwehr-Holland bureau hoodwinked both SOE in London and the Dutch government in exile, transmitting information – not all of which was false – and making enquiries concerning the arrival of agents and arms drops. At the end of that time the Dutch officials and SOE requested that Jambroes return to Britain.

Major Giskes, Chief of Section III-F of Abwehr-Holland, in conjunction with SS Sturmbannführer (Lieutenant-Colonel) Joseph Schreider of the SD, faced a dilemma. Obviously Jambroes, at that time in a German prison (and later executed at Mauthausen), could not visit Britain. On the other hand he had aides in Holland who, while known to SOE at least by name, could make the trip. It was accordingly suggested that an aide named Captain Kist, a Dutch officer serving SOE, could be substituted for Jambroes. Kist was also in a German prison, but this was not known in London. The Abwehr scheme was for no one actually to go to Britain but to satisfy the British that in fact Jambroes' aide would be available for the trip, in order to encourage SOE to be available for substantiation if it were required.

Captain Kist was not widely known in underground circles even in Holland. Major Giskes was confident that he could create a successful impersonation, and he did.

The *England Spiel* contact argued about Kist returning instead of Jambroes, but in the end London accepted Kist as a substitute. He would undertake the journey in the company of a Belgian Resistance leader.

The man chosen to impersonate Kist was a German Abwehr sergeant named Karl Boden who was fluent in Dutch. The Belgian Resistance chieftain was Sonderführer (Group Leader) Richard Christmann, who spoke excellent French.

The Abwehr's purpose in all this was simple. In order for the various underground organizations to get agents in and out of Europe, perfected escape routes were required. The Germans knew about the Spanish connection; they in fact controlled it. They did not know much about the French routes, which had been very successful. Accordingly Kist and the Belgian did not use the Spanish road. They went directly to Paris, arriving there on 18 May 1943, and with information from Abwehr sources were able to contact several French *résistants* who, it turned out, were members of a thriving underground association called 'Prosper'.

For German Military Intelligence this development nearly eclipsed the original assignment of Boden and Christmann.

The impersonators met Jack and Francine Agazarian, a team of husband and wife, plus Andrée Borel and Gilbert Norman, all of whom were SOE agents. The Germans were convincing. As counter-intelligence agents they knew how to use their knowledge of the underground to leave excellent impressions.

They accumulated an extensive list of Prosper circuit's members. Before they were finished, they had also uncovered other secret Resistance groups, either known to Prosper's people or casually mentioned during conversations.

The German list grew.

During the course of arrangements for an aircraft to pick up the pair of impersonators, the Germans were supplied with an address where Prosper members could be contacted. They were also advised to return to Holland and wait until they received word that the air-lift which was to get them out of France had been arranged.

Neither Boden nor Christmann left Paris. They brought their lists up to date even as several additional SOE agents were arriving in France by air, foredoomed participants in the débâcle to follow.

These were Charles Skepper, Cecily Lefort, Diana Rowden and an exotic creature named Noor Inayat Khan. Skepper was subsequently executed at the Hamburg Gestapo prison; Cecily Lefort was captured during a raid on a Resistance headquarters at Montelimar; Diana Rowden was killed at Natzweiler by phenol injection, and Noor Inayat Khan, whose mother's name was Ora Baker and whose father was an Indian mystic of the Sufi sect, was captured, sent to Dachau, tortured and put to death. (Her training résumé had said she was unfit for clandestine work.)

These were only part of the Prosper circuit who were captured. Major Francis Suttill, head of Prosper, was hanged at Sachsenhausen on 19 March 1945; Gilbert Norman, Suttill's deputy, after a brief stint as a collaborator, was sent to Mauthausen concentration camp where he was shot on 6 September 1944. Andrée Borel was put to death by poison injection at Natzweiler. Yvonne Rudelatt, whose code-name in the Prosper circuit had been Jacqueline, spent some time at Ravensbrück, then was sent to the extermination camp at Belsen where she was put to death in the gas chamber. Two Canadian SOE agents, McAlister and Pickersgill, were sent to Buchenwald extermination camp marked for *Nacht und Nebel* (literally 'night and fog', meaning they were to be put to death without record). Both were hanged on 4 October 1944.

Boden and Christmann had acquitted themselves quite well. But their initial assignment, to infiltrate the air-lift project, was less successful, for while they uncovered a number of secret landing fields, the Lysander aircraft used for this service were so light they could land almost anywhere. They continued to operate successfully until the end of the war, the most elusive aeroplanes of the Royal Air Force.

The information Boden and Christmann uncovered concerning other *réseaux* was subsequently developed until, as with falling dominoes, the destruction of the Prosper organization led to additional Resistance groups being uncovered and destroyed. The number of French and SOE associates put to death was large. In fact SOE's high percentage of fatalities was excessive even for an organization engaged as it was, against foemen who were easily SOE's match. SOE F Section records revealed that, of 480 agents who served in France, 26 survived captivity and 106 were either put to death by the Germans or killed resisting arrest. That was only for F section.

Comparative losses for other sections, the Dutch, Norwegian, Belgian and Danish sections raised the total of lost, never to return, or recorded as dead, to an inordinately high percentage of agents sent to the Continent.

But what happened in France was almost a side issue of what occurred in Holland as a result of the capture of Joseph Jambroes. There, in the great cities of the Netherlands, one of the most incredible Intelligence *coups* of the war was guided to success under the aegis of Major Giskes of the Abwehr and Lieutenant-Colonel Joseph Schreieder of the Sicherheitsdienst in a unique example of co-operation between rival counter-intelligence agencies.

13

An Abwehr *Coup*

Like the other nations of Europe overrun by the Germans, Holland was in a state of bewilderment and disarray. Beginning with the German occupation in 1940, the country was without leadership. When Queen Wilhelmina fled to London, her escape supervised by a former commissioner of police at The Hague, F. van't Sant, she left behind nothing but the will of her people to resist. Dutch Intelligence had made no provision for clandestine organizations, not even secret radio stations. The Queen and her government in exile were completely isolated from Holland, and although a few members of the Dutch Secret Services arrived in Britain with Wilhelmina's entourage, they had no links with their homeland.

Nor was British Intelligence much better off. In its equally hasty departure, an agent of SIS abandoned an attaché case in which were filed the names and addresses of all his Dutch associates. This was discovered by the Germans, with sanguinary results.

Former commissioner van't Sant, who became the Queen's secretary in London, undertook the creation of a Dutch secret service, with assistance from Britain's Secret Intelligence Service. This occurred in the midsummer of 1940, at about the same time that SOE was conceived, but van't Sant's Centrale Inlichtingendienst (Central Intelligence Service) became operative that same summer while SOE did not have a functioning Dutch Section until much later.

In fact van't Sant's Central Intelligence Service, in co-operation with SIS, sent its first spy to Holland that same summer.

It was a case of misguided enthusiasm, for while van't Sant had learned that an organization called Orde Dienst, an embryonic nationalist group, was in process of being formed, his ignorance of Hitler's counter-intelligence service was profound. The Dutch Intelligence Services had of course been aware of Germany's espionage capability before the invasion. What they had considerably less knowledge of was German counter-intelligence proficiency.

The first Dutch agent sent back was a naval lieutenant named Lodo van Hamel. He was air-dropped near Leyden on the night of 28 August 1940. Van Hamel brought with him a wireless set and plans for organizing underground espionage groups.

He originally had indifferent success. Many Dutchmen he contacted refused to become involved. But van Hamel persevered and eventually, after two months of effort, managed to establish four small groups. These were able to contact London by duplicating the wireless set he had arrived with.

Van Hamel met with Orde Dienst members and eventually accumulated a list of German military posts, airfields and coastal defence installations. Much of this information was on microfilm. A leader of the Orde Dienst. Baas Becking, agreed to accompany van Hamel on his return to London and accordingly gathered more documents. These included codes and copies of German reports and orders, as well as photographs. Becking filled a suitcase with these things to take with him.

Van Hamel contacted van't Sant and was told to go with Becking to the Friesland hamlet of Zurig, near where the North Sea paralleled the Zuider Zee. He and Becking would be picked up by a British seaplane on the night of 14 September. A pair of Orde Dienst partisans, a man and a woman, were to accompany van Hamel and Becking as guides.

The group arrived on the west coast of Friesland near Zurig while it was still daylight and were seen by an SD V-man whose interest – and suspicion – was aroused. In that isolated area people did not normally stroll the dikes carrying suitcases, unless of course they were to be met by a boat – or an aeroplane.

The V-man reported to his superior, who immediately despatched a squad of German police to make the arrest and subsequently sent a teletype message to the office of Sicherheitsdienst commandant Colonel Wilhelm Harstner at The Hague stating that 'a British agent who calls himself van Dalen was apprehended . . . in [the] company of three other persons while awaiting a British sea plane . . .'

Standartenführer Harstner ordered Lieutenant-Colonel Joseph Schreieder, who had recently assumed command of the SD's Amt IV counter-intelligence department in Holland, to make the investigation.

Schreieder, who a month earlier had been transferred from Austria, took two SD men with him and went to the AST office at Leeuwarden where the prisoners were being detained.

The woman and three men were interrogated. No incriminating documents were found on them because van Hamel and Becking had thrown their suitcases into the water when they had seen the German policemen approaching. (The valises were eventually recovered by the Germans.)

All four prisoners were taken to the SD's offices at The Hague, where additional interrogation ensued. Lieutenant van Hamel admitted his true identity and that he was a secret agent of the Dutch government in London but said that neither of the Orde Dienst guides knew anything about his espionage activities and that Baas Becking had come along in order to hitch a ride to Britain, from where he intended to fly to the Dutch East Indies to join his family. Becking and the two partisans were released. Lieutenant van Hamel was eventually tried before a German military court on charges of espionage, was sentenced to death and in June 1941 was executed.

By that time, the early summer of 1941, Special Operations Executive had a Dutch section, and van't Sant's Central Intelligence Service, profiting from the loss of Lodo van Hamel, concentrated on exploiting its wireless link with the homeland.

There were additional reasons why the Dutch were wary of sending out other agents. Information from Holland convincingly portrayed German counter-intelligence as superior to anything the Allies could oppose it with. There was also a geographical barrier. The Dutch coast was accessible to German sea patrols and was under constant surveillance. Delivering spies by sea was practically impossible. As for air-drops, for much of the year sea-girt Holland was subject to heavy fogs which did not dissipate for weeks at a time.

Nor at this time was the Dutch Resistance movement able to do much more than occupy itself with radio contact with Britain and work out problems of organization. The Orde Dienst, for example, was appropriately named. It meant

'Order Service'. Founded by former officers of the Dutch armed services, its original purpose was to maintain order after liberation. It was not initially organized for either espionage or subversion, and early efforts to include it in a co-ordinated underground network to serve those functions was not an immediate success.

More pressingly relevant was a group called the 'Beggars' Action' movement. It pre-dated the Orde Dienst and was more vigorous in its opposition to the occupation. At its headquarters, a boat club, an assortment of students, businessmen, ex-officers of the Dutch armed forces and newsmen put out a clandestine newspaper, harassed the Germans and generally demonstrated aggressive opposition, but they were inept in their attempts at creating a workable espionage-sabotage network. A leader of the Beggars was Bernard Ijzerdraat. He, like the others, learned too late how priceless good security was. In their quest for members they recruited a number of people who belonged to Adriaan Mussert's Dutch Nazi Party. The SD counter-intelligence moved swiftly. Ijzerdraat and nearly all the other Beggars' officers were captured; subsequently fifteen of them were put before a German firing squad, and the Beggars' organization was destroyed.

Additional Resistance groups in Holland included the Communists, the Catholics and the Socialists, but because they all lacked experience and were initially unable to contact London, their contributions were negligible. Basically, what the Dutch Resistance movement lacked was knowledgeable leadership and the sense of co-operation without which it could not hope to oppose the Germans successfully. The will to resist was there, and it became stronger as time passed, but nationalism, like heroism, was no substitute for knowledgeability or practical, cold-blooded experience, and these things were lacking.

It was this inability among the Dutch to organize effectively that made the work of the German counter-intelligence agencies relatively simple. It also helped that Hitler's attitude toward the Dutch was lenient, and although the Gestapo handled counter-espionage, by an agreement between Himmler and Reichskommissar Seyss-Inqurt, the customary Gestapo brutality was held to a minimum.

At this time, the winter of 1940, the Abwehr had only a

small staff in Holland, at The Hague, and as Military Intelligence it was assigned to the headquarters of the German Commander-in-Chief, Luftwaffe General Friedrich Christiansen.

After a popular uprising in early 1941, sparked by scarcity of food, inflationary prices and persecution of Dutch Jews, the SD and Gestapo organizations were greatly increased; at the same time German administrators, including SS Obergruppenführer Hans Rauter, the Gestapo's commissioner of public safety, altered the policy of leniency.

The Abwehr office, supervised by a Colonel Hempel, while of course concerned with counter-intelligence, had not to this time in Holland had much reason to expand its internal investigative procedures, and, unlike the Gestapo and SD, the Abwehr had no police force to engage in field work, nor had any such function been envisioned for Military Intelligence. Therefore, after the popular uprising of February 1941, the Gestapo, which was essentially a police-oriented organization, not only made the arrests and did the field work but also engaged in the counter-intelligence investigative procedures which led to the police work, and this, in Abwehr eyes, was a violation of Abwehr prerogatives.

And yet, because Military Intelligence did not have a police unit of its own, when an Abwehr counter-intelligence investigation resulted in the need for a physical apprehension, the Abwehr was obliged to call for help from either the SD or the Gestapo.

In the early winter of 1941, the expanded and reinforced Gestapo in Holland caused anxiety in the Abwehr. When Lieutenant-Colonel Joseph Schreieder, made confident and assertive after his success in the Lodo van Hamel affair, assumed broader counter-intelligence powers, the Abwehr Tirpitzufer directorate decided to augment Colonel Hempel's staff at The Hague with an officer capable of countering Schreieder and the Gestapo.

He was Major Herman Giskes, formerly of the Abwehr headquarters in Paris. He was a counter-intelligence specialist serving under Colonel (later Major-General) von Bentivegni's Section III (security, counter-intelligence and counter-sabotage). Giskes was a tall, sturdy, balding man, pleasant, cultured, keenly intelligent, with a sense of humour, an ability to get along with people, and while giving an impression of easy, almost casual good nature, he was an individual of great energy and subtlety.

It would be reasonable to assume that, when Admiral Canaris approved of Giskes' transfer to The Hague, he did so confident that the appointment would provide Abwehr-Holland with the perfect foil for Schreieder and the Gestapo. But Herman Giskes did more; he accomplished something few Abwehr officers ever achieved, an excellent working part-nership with the rival SD.

He managed this despite a judgement of Joseph Schreieder which was bare of all illusions. After their first meeting he had this to say about Schreieder: 'A small, almost bald man with a heavy, round head, in the uniform of an SS Sturmbannführer, entered my office. He extended a flabby, well-manicured hand . . . His age was difficult to judge – perhaps forty.' (Close enough; at this time Joseph Schreieder was thirty-nine.) 'Slightly protruding, rat-like eyes gave life to a pasty face, and the nose betrayed the delights of the bottle. The whole well-fed man exuded joviality, his slightly provincial accent emphasiz-ing the note of southern warmth, as though he was immensely pleased to have found in me an entirely unexpected and beloved old friend. He radiated the well-known benevolence of certain criminal investigators . . . To judge from his intimate manner and the friendly "*Lieber Kamerad Giskes*", with which he continually addressed me, I realized it was not going to be very difficult . . .'

Nor was it, but first Herman Giskes had to set his new department in order. He moved the office to the Dutch seaside town of Scheveningen, adjacent to German Naval Headquar-ters on the outskirts of The Hague, to a building screened by lime trees so that visitors could enter without undue notice.

At about this same time a Dutch Resistance group under the aegis of a Rotterdam lawyer named Johan Stijkel, and two former Dutch military officers, Colonel J. P. Bolten and Major-General H. D. S. Hasselman, was coming into prominence. Through a wireless expert, Cornelis Drupsteen, the Stijkel group contacted SIS and engaged in radio communication with London.

In the spring of 1941 Johan Stijkel contacted SIS with a proposal that he and three associates visit London to deliver information which had been gathered subsequent to the failure of the van Hamel mission. SIS was agreeable, so Stijkel advised that he and his companions would leave Holland in a small boat, trusting in a rendezvous at sea with the British.

It was prohibited for Dutchmen, mostly fishermen, to leave the mainland without clearance from the harbour police, but this created no problem. Stijkel knew a pair of Dutch harbour officers who had been associated with Resistance groups. Both were V-men employed by the SD in penetrating underground organizations.

On the night of 2 April Johan Stijkel, his aide Jan Gude and the brothers van der Plas, with their incriminating papers, boarded the fishing boat ready to put to sea. A squad of SS men appeared on the landing, while several motor launches filled with other members of the SS blockaded the boat.

The prisoners were taken to Gestapo headquarters at The Hague and interrogated. The result was that all the members of the Stijkel group were rounded up and sent to Berlin for trial. All were sentenced to death and executed. One member was not shot but apparently died in prison; he never returned to Holland, at any rate.

This *coup* was supervised by Joseph Schreieder, and as with the van Hamel affair, it not only heightened Schreieder's standing with his superior, Colonel Harstner, but strengthened the SD's prestige at the Abwehr's expense.

Schreieder had other irons in the fire, which had become necessary as the Resistance movement in Holland gathered momentum, and despite Herman Giskes' unflattering opinion of him, Joseph Schreieder was experienced in the subtleties of his vocation. During the summer of 1941 Schreieder learned through one of his V-men, Antonius van der Waals, of the existence of an underground radio station which was regularly transmitting to London. Because van der Waals could not pinpoint the location of the transmitter beyond saying that it was near the town of Bilthoven, Schreieder appealed to the Abwehr for assistance and a Funkhorchdienst radio-detection van was provided. It toured the Utrecht-Bilthoven area for some time, unable to locate the transmitter because it operated at irregular intervals and only for brief periods, but the area was ultimately confined, and finally the residence of a Dutch businessman named Jan Siringa was put under constant surveillance. When the clandestine transmitter went on the air, the Germans struck. They not only captured a young Dutch agent serving in SIS but found a complete radio post in a shed. The Dutch agent, Hans Zomer, also had in his possession codes and their keys. Schreieder, more impressed with the discovery and capture, gave the unintelligible papers to an SD sergeant, Ernst May, and took his prisoner to Gestapo headquarters for interrogation. Sergeant May, intrigued by the coded messages, tried to decipher them. He had no training as a cryptanalyst, which makes his achievement all the more extraordinary. He not only deciphered the messages but discovered the security check with which every clandestine radio-operator was provided. Without that check impersonation was practically impossible; with it a transmitter could be 'turned around'.

Hanz Zomer was adamant in his refusal to co-operate with the Gestapo. They tried everything from torture to hypnosis.

Sergeant May, meanwhile, went to Schreieder to explain how he had broken the codes. Schreieder was not interested. May told Schreieder that with the security check Zomer's radio could be used to dupe the British and that it could also be used to contact and uncover other clandestine transmitting stations. Schreieder was still not interested.

A few months later another Resistance cell was penetrated by a V-man, and among those captured was a former radio-man of the Royal Dutch Navy, William van der Reyden, in whose possession was found another set of codes. As before, the Gestapo was more concerned with destroying a Resistance group than it was with the documents taken during the raid, but Sergeant May cultivated van der Reyden and, as a post-war Board of Inquiry noted, 'From ... van der Reyden's information, Sergeant May was in a position to increase his knowledge of the code, used by British SOE agents, by an appreciable degree. Van der Reyden revealed not only the general code but also details relating to his particular case. Moreover van der Reyden put May in possession of facts concerning a special security measure, the so-called test question ...'

Lieutenant-Colonel Schreieder finally became interested in exploiting the two radio posts in Gestapo possession, and meanwhile Major Giskes, through an Abwehr investigation, was moving towards the same goal. Some time before Schreieder's raid which resulted in the capture of William van der Reyden, an Abwehr sergeant, Willy Kupp, prevailed upon Giskes to meet with a former Dutch reserve officer named George Ridderhof. Giskes was not enthusiastic. Ridderhof's record indicated that the man was under investigation by the German currency control bureau for black-market operations. He was a professional renegade whose exploits included opium-smuggling and grand theft.

George Ridderhof was a large, fat man who walked with a limp, drank periodically and had a large acquaintanceship in the Amsterdam underworld. He met Giskes at the American Hotel and told him he knew a member of the Dutch underground who was in contact with a pair of British spies, and if he were put in Abwehr employ and protected from the imminent prosecution which he felt sure would result in a conviction for black-marketing, he would serve German Military Intelligence.

Giskes, always interested in acquiring V-men, gave Ridderhof the designation of Agent F2087, code-named him 'George' and moved to have the currency control bureau's charges held in abeyance. In return Ridderhof filed a report stating that an air-drop was being arranged and that 'A widespread (underground) organization is being planned, which is to be systematically trained and armed.'

Giskes was sceptical. Still, there was one way to prove whether Ridderhof was lying or not. Giskes wanted the date of the air-drop and its location.

Ridderhof eventually supplied both. He had penetrated an Orde Dienst group by cultivating a former captain of the Dutch armed forces named van den Berg. The two 'British' spies Ridderhof had mentioned to Giskes were Dutch nationals, Huburtus Lauwers and Thijs Taconis, in the employ of SOE. They had parachuted into Holland some months earlier to work at co-ordinating the various Resistance organizations. Behind their assignment was a scheme of which neither Lauwers nor Taconis probably had any inkling at the time. It was

called *Plan Holland* and had the full support of the Allied
Chiefs of Staff. It was similar to the plan then going forward in
France to organize, arm and co-ordinate a secret army. Upon
the success of these plans depended to a considerable extent
the Allied ability to return to the Continent. The Allied
General Staff was in fact planning strategy which included
large armed forces of nationalists whose purpose would be to
delay reinforcements for the German armies of defence when
an Allied invasion occurred. *Plan Holland*, had it succeeded,
might have swayed the Allies to strike along the Dutch coast
rather than, as they did, along the French coast. The reason it
did not succeed went back to Agent F2087 and his Abwehr
employer.

Lauwers, serving as Taconis's radio-operator, was transmitting from the rooms of a former Dutch Army officer on
Fahrenheit Street in The Hague. Funkhorchdienst vans had
already detected clandestine transmissions between London
and The Hague and were in the process of locating the local
transmitter. Ridderhof told Giskes that the van den Berg group
was being instructed from London through the BBC's European division, which was at Bush House on the Strand.
Normally these broadcasts, heard throughout Europe between 7.30 and 9 p.m., were prefaced by the first measure of
Beethoven's Fifth Symphony, V-for-Victory. They were in
coded language and offered personal messages as well as instructions, and although it was strictly forbidden for people in
the occupied countries to listen almost everyone who possessed a radio did listen, including people belonging to the Resistance such as members of the van den Berg network to whom
they were especially pertinent. The Germans also listened.

For the Germans the difficulty arose from their inability to
break the BBC's codes, so, while they heard what they knew
had to be instructions to the European underground, they
could do little. Herman Giskes' exasperation in this regard was
mitigated when Ridderhof told him that van den Berg had been
told in a BBC broadcast that there would be an air-drop near
Hooghalen during the last week of February. The code number
indicating that the drop would occur was 962. On the afternoon of 27 February this number was repeated several times
during a BBC broadcast.

Giskes called for police action to secure the area of the drop, and when an RAF aircraft appeared above Hooghalen at midnight, jettisoned several large containers attached to parachutes, then vanished, the German police who were guarding all the access roads remained in place. It had not been Giskes's plan to arrest the partisans who retrieved the containers (one of which was carried out of the territory by wind). Ridderhof was among them. Giskes wanted his V-men thoroughly accepted by the underground members of van den Berg's organization.

The following day Ridderhof met Giskes with an account of the air-dropped supplies. They consisted of handguns, explosives and ammunition. There was one final item to report. The partisans had been led by a tall man referred to as 'Long Thijs' by the others. Giskes had little difficulty in identifying 'Long Thijs' as Thijs Taconis. He accomplished this identification through a V-man named Droog who had penetrated an Orde Dienst at Arnhem where Droog had got to know Taconis.

Unlike Joseph Schreieder, Major Giskes wanted a Resistance wireless set and codes more than he wanted to capture a few *résistants*. When he heard from the Funkhorchdienst that they had located the clandestine transmitter on Fahrenheit Street, he went to the Binnenhof headquarters of the Gestapo to solicit field assistance in making the raid. Joseph Schreieder was co-operative. Giskes had the address of van den Berg's residence from Ridderhof, as well as the location of the Arnhem cell. Between them Giskes and Schreieder devised a plan for decimating the Orde Dienst.

On 6 March 1942, a Friday, Huburtus Lauwers was awaiting his scheduled time to transmit – 6 p.m. His host, the former Dutch Army officer, Lieutenant Teller, whose rooms Lauwers had been transmitting from on Fahrenheit Street, warned Lauwers that he had seen several official German cars parked at a nearby crossroads. One of the cars contained a German Lieutenant Heinrich and several of his Funkhorchdienst technicians. The other car had contained Major Giskes and Sergeant Willy Kupp. Now Kupp was down Fahrenheit Street where he could watch the Teller residence.

At precisely six o'clock Huburtus Lauwers began signalling London. He was initially required to fine-tune his transmitter, and one of Lieutenant Heinrich's men in the first car immediately picked up the transmission on a detection-finding instrument.

Schreieder and his Gestapo squad still had not arrived. Suddenly, Lauwers stopped transmitting. It seemed probable to Major Giskes that something had alarmed Lauwers, and he decided to stage the raid without Schreieder. He was preparing to approach the house when three carloads of armed men appeared on Fahrenheit Street and stopped at the Teller residence.

Inside, the Tellers and Lauwers tried to hide the transmitter by lowering it from a window to a flowerbed. Like most desperate improvisations, this was not a very good one.

Lauwers snatched up the written messages he had been about to transmit from, pocketed them, told Teller to accompany him and left the house by a rear doorway. They gained the street and began walking away. They were easily overtaken.

Both men were returned to the house, where Lieutenant Heinrich's men were examining Lauwers' wireless set with considerable interest. Shortly afterwards the Tellers and Lauwers were taken to the Gestapo prison at Scheveningen and after interrogation were put in cells. At Major Giskes' suggestion, Huburtus Lauwers was held in solitary confinement for almost a week.

When Giskes returned to the 'Citadel', his name for the office at the Hoogeweg adjacent to German Naval Headquarters, he learned that Captain van den Berg had been seized along with several members of his group, and from Arnhem there was information that Thijs Taconis's residence was under surveillance, and the moment he appeared the field police would arrest him, which eventually occurred, but not without incident. Thijs Taconis was a large man who hated Germans and was capable of violence.

Lieutenant Colonel Schreieder was pleased. He had a number of SOE spies. Major Giskes was also quite satisfied. He had an intact clandestine transmitter and the coded messages Huburtus Lauwers had been about to use in transmitting to London. He also had the broken codes of Sergeant May. From this source it was possible to decode Lauwers' messages, one of which stated that the German battleship *Prinz Eugen*, which the Royal Navy was particularly anxious to find, was in drydock at Schiedem for repairs.

Major Giskes was in no hurry. When he finally visited Lauwers, he told the SOE agent 'forcefully, that he alone could save himself and Thijs . . . from a death sentence by a German military court . . .' To do this, Giskes said, Lauwers 'would have to transmit . . . the messages which he had been unable to pass on when he had been arrested'.

Lauwers showed interest, and suspicion. The messages were harmful to the Germans. Why would they want him to transmit them? What Giskes wanted was for German telegraphers to watch Lauwers as he transmitted. Every wireless operator had individual characteristics. Lauwers could only be impersonated successfully if his style was faithfully duplicated. Also, there were the security checks; each SOE radioman had a secret way of letting London know if he was transmitting under duress. He committed certain letters, certain numbers, or added words which in London were warnings. Sergeant May had uncovered the security checks of Hans Zomer; Giskes now had to accomplish the same thing with Huburtus Lauwers.

But the captive refused to co-operate. Giskes told him the code had been broken. He would not believe it. He was also told that Taconis was in custody, and he refused to believe that either. Taconis was produced, in handcuffs. So also was a leader of the van den Berg group, Jacob van Dijk. Finally Giskes placed before Lauwers the decoded message about the *Prinz Eugen*.

Lauwers yielded, not to save his life but because he had only one chance left to warn SOE – his security checks. Cannily, he told the Germans about some security checks, but not all of them.

An attempt to get Thijs Taconis to join Giskes' *England Spiel* resulted in total failure. When one of Taconis's SS guards tried physical coercion, the Dutchman beat him senseless. After that Taconis was kept securely chained. (He was executed at Mauthausen in the early winter of 1944.)

Huburtus Lauwers began transmitting under German control. He continued to do this for two years, constantly trying to warn SOE through security checks. After the war SOE excused its two-year blunder on the grounds that it had assumed Lauwers was transmitting under other than normal circumstances, therefore his messages were not questioned – *for two years*!

It was not the messages Lauwers transmitted – all careful German fabrications – which were important. It was the messages he received. He was informed, for example, that a secret agent named Lieutenant Arnold Baatsen would be parachuted at an underground drop-zone north of Assen the night of 27 March. Baatsen, a professional photographer, was dropped on schedule. George Ridderhof was in charge of the supposed Resistance men who were to welcome Baatsen. Major Giskes and Lieutenant-Colonel Schreieder were waiting in a nearby parked car. When Baatsen landed, along with several containers of explosives and weapons, the *résistants*, all V-men, escorted him to the parked car where he was greeted by an Abwehr major and an SS Sturmbannführer. He was handcuffed and led away.

Giskes subsequently had Lauwers notify SOE that Baatsen had arrived safely, and that was the beginning.

But by this time, the closing months of 1941 to the autumn of 1942, secret agents were arriving quite regularly, along with drops of weapons.

The United States was Britain's armed ally. The power of those opposing Germany on the Continent was increasing, and this growth was reflected in the number of secret agents arriving in Europe, as well as in the stockpiles of weapons being supplied to the Resistance groups, who were also recruiting members in great numbers.

In Berlin, Germany's gentlemen with the claret stripes down their trouser legs, unable to restrain Hitler and so far at least unwilling either to remove or to assassinate him, had no illusions about the nation being in the path of another two-front war.

In the Netherlands, a relative backwater, with the Allies' *Plan Holland* still vitally important, the Intelligence commands were preparing to embark upon their own campaign of attrition.

14

Giskes-Spiel

On 5 April German police found a dead parachutist whose papers identified him as Henk Martens. Neither the Abwehr nor the SD had any information about him, which signified that British Intelligence was not clearing all agents through the Lauwers contact.

It was reasonable to assume this, and in fact it was the truth. Piet Homberg arrived in the autumn of 1941, Lieutenant Leonard Andringa arrived on 10 March 1942, the other half of the team of which Henk Martens had been the radioman. On 29 March another team, Hendrich Jordaan and Gerard Ras, arrived at night by parachute. About a week later another pair from SOE, Hendrick Sebes and Berend Kloos, were air-dropped. Two weeks later Lieutenant Hendrick van Haas came by sea, landing safely at Castricum.

SOE, believing it had ten agents undetected in Holland, was prepared to increase its air-drops of weapons and explosives. Without realizing it, although by now it should have, since Huburtus Lauwers had repeatedly transmitted warnings, SOE had, along with several freshly arrived radio links, an Achilles heel which would destroy them all.

Lieutenant van Haas had arrived with an instrument for ground-to-air communication, and SOE particularly wanted to contact him so that future clandestine flights could be guided in.

Van Haas, whose code-name was 'Pilj' (arrow), was directed to the safe house of a Haarlem tobacconist named F. J. Martens – through Lauwers' wireless.

Major Giskes passed this information along to Joseph Schreieder, who despatched one of his best V-men, Leo Poos, to the tobacco shop. Poos, posing as a member of the Resistance, gained the tobacconist's confidence and learned about the other agents.

In rapid succession Piet Homberg and van Haas were captured. On 9 May Sebes and Jordaan were taken, along with their wireless set. George Dessing, an SIS agent, was nearly captured but escaped through a window of the men's bathroom at a café when German police arrived. But Giskes knew his haunts and ordered them put under surveillance. Dessing did not return to them. He began a nightmare escape from Holland which got him to neutral Spain, eventually, and there he was incarcerated. He finally reached London in the autumn of 1943 nearly half a year after escaping from Holland. His report to SOE was treated with scepticism. The transmissions to Lauwers and the other controlled radios were continued!

Jordaan, who had been instructing a Resistance man as a wireless-operator, did as Huburtus Lauwers had done: he agreed to operate his wireless set for the Abwehr in order to slip through the security checks and warn London. He did this during a transmission asking permission to use his trainee radio-operator. Again, the security checks were ignored. The Germans were elated when London radioed back for Jordaan's new operator to send test signals. Giskes used a German radioman to reply to London. The answer arrived: 'Instruct new operator in use of security checks.' Following this came the secret combination itself!

Major Giskes now had three captured radios, with codes and security checks. He acquired two more when Schreieder's V-man Leo Poos discovered, through the tobacco shop, that eleven members of the Resistance, including Piet Homberg's brother, planned to flee to Britain by boat. On the night of 17 May, with Poos watching, the partisans put to sea. Within moments German patrol craft appeared. The partisans' boat was machine-gunned, nearly all its occupants were wounded, and after the vessel was towed to shore, the partisans were sent to Scheveningen prison. The radios from the boat were delivered to the Abwehr office.

Not many days later, SOE-London advised Lauwers that two more agents, Antony Steen and Herman Parlevliet, would arrive shortly, with radio equipment and another ground-to-air communication instrument. Lauwers, still trying frantically to warn London, even interposed the word 'caught' in his messages. It was ignored.

When Steen and Parlevliet arrived, they landed among armed German police. It was no longer necessary to use V-men impersonating partisans.

The Giskes-Schreieder association continued to prosper. Through the captured transmitters, using correct codes and observing every SOE rule, it was possible not only to confirm the arrival of agents but to fabricate reports of success among the Resistance groups. Over a period of time an illusion was created that a formidable secret army was being organized, when in fact there was no such thing, and in order to flush-out this story the Germans requested additional supplies, guns, medical supplies, explosives, radio equipment, even cigarettes and money.

SOE sent it all, and meanwhile the captures continued to occur. On 23 May Felix Ort, a radioman for a cell in The Hague, was uncovered through V-man van der Waals. Ort was taken with his wireless set. Another radioman, Evert Radema, was caught on 29 May. Between V-men and what was learned from captives, the SOE network was being decimated by the law of falling dominoes.

Lauwers, still desperately trying to warn London, had no success whatsoever.

On 23 June SOE agents Johannes Buizer and Jan van Reitschoten landed at the field near Assen where Giskes and Schreieder had waited in a parked car for Arnold Baatsen more than a year before, and the same ordeal awaited them. Both were captured while still in their parachute harness, with their radios and codes.

The Abwehr now controlled SOE's radio link with Holland. There were several transmitters still at large, but with six 'turned-around' radios, complete with operators and security checks, the bulk of the clandestine work was handled through German counter-intelligence. Instructions from London arrived almost daily. A captured agent named Gerard Hemert brought with him instructions for Thijs Taconis to dynamite the German naval installation at Kootwijk. Taconis had by then been a prisoner for almost half a year. Radio instructions for agents to destroy other facilities resulted in reinforcements being sent to those places. The nature of the instructions was revealing: reports were requested concerning the progress of *Plan Holland*'s secret army. It was easy to invent encouraging replies. SOE had no way to verify the false reports except through the 'burned' transmitters and their German-controlled operators, and the Germans learned all they had to know about *Plan Holland*.

Giskes' 'Citadel' had to increase its staff to handle the immense amount of paperwork engendered by the success of the Major's *England-Spiel*. It was never routine work. Upon a number of occasions the Abwehr came face to face with dilemmas, as when an enquiry from the SOE's Baker Street office requested information concerning the progress of an agent the Abwehr knew nothing about. Out and out prevarication was dangerous. It could arouse suspicion and destroy the entire Abwehr operation.

Major Giskes chose the middle course: he cautiously requested additional information and when that arrived it enabled him to cull through the SOE prisoners for an agent who had been associated with the missing spy. Information from this source made it possible for Giskes to reconstruct a believable pastiche.

The danger of an uncaught agent discovering the truth certainly existed, but the nature of the work being highly secret, so secret in fact that agents were not told about other agents, minimized this risk.

In the larger view, the Abwehr achievement destroyed *Plan Holland*, the Allied scheme which, coupled with another idea, *Plan Roundup*, was to ensure that a well-armed underground army would arise when the Allies landed near Le Havre and began a drive across the Meuse into Belgium and Holland, or, if it proved feasible, landed on the Dutch coast for a thrust into Germany proper by the back door.

What the Abwehr learned of these things resulted in German reinforcements being sent not only into Holland for coastal defence but also to Belgium and all along the much longer coast of France from Dunkirk on around to the vicinity of the Channel Islands.

But in itself this was to some degree self-defeating. Germany was straining every resource in the East where Hitler's 'six months campaign' was chewing up armies and supplies on an unprecedented scale. Beefing up defences in the West could only contribute to a weakening in the East.

But in the lesser view, that of scotching Field Marshal Sir Alan Brook's pet project, *Plan Holland*, the Abwehr had succeeded so well that, had the Allies landed in 1942 relying on a Dutch secret army to block the Rhine, destroy communications between Holland and other occupied territories, and stall German reinforcements until an invincible Allied lodgement was secured, there would without much doubt have been a disaster of such magnitude that the Allies might never have been able to recover from it.

To the later allegation that in 1942 the Allies could not have invaded the Continent because they were too weak and disorganized, it should be pointed out in rebuttal that *Plan Holland*, like *Sledgehammer* or *Jael*, or even *Overlord*, did not have a date for consummation. In the case of the Netherlands in 1942 there could have been no fixed date for an uprising. There was no way of knowing when, or if, a large Resistance army would be operational, but the best guess, even if the Abwehr had not successfully intervened, would have been at least one year and more likely two years.

But the planning went forward, as it had to do, and as it revealed an increasingly aggressive character, German concern mounted. A query from London respecting the possibility of high-level assassinations, which began with the words, 'In our opinion the time has come to begin active hostilities . . .', worried both Giskes and Schreieder. This message requested confirmation from the underground that it was prepared to comply, and ended with the statement that '. . . when you are ready we will send you a first list . . .'

Giskes requested the names, and they were supplied. Most of the intended victims were Dutch Nazis, a few such as an SS Commander, Colonel Feldmeyer, were Germans, but the implication was that this first list might be a test. If it was, then the lists to follow would certainly contain more German names. It was known, too, that high among British Intelligence's priorities was elimination of such notorious SS and Gestapo officials as General Hans Rauter, Holland's General Commissar of Public Safety, a brutal administrator whose ruthlessness had been demonstrated during both the popular uprising of February 1941 and the nearly simultaneous persecution of Dutch Jews.

The Gestapo had always been a special target of Allied assassins. Joseph Schreieder had cause for anxiety. He and Herman Giskes sent separate reports to their superiors. Schreieder's superior, Colonel Wilhelm Harstner, SD Commander in Holland, notified Rauter. Giskes' information went directly to General von Bentivegni in Berlin, where it was also seen by Admiral Canaris.

The solution rested with the Abwehr's *England-Spiel*, which would obtain the names of proposed victims, and with Joseph Schreieder's field police who would provide protection for them.

Also, the co-ordinated efforts of both SD and Abwehr V-men in uncovering more Resistance groups, and the apprehension at drop-zones of additional SOE agents, would lessen the peril, although nothing could eliminate it entirely, but then the assassination of Germans in occupied countries had always been a risk, so an occasional success, as with Reinhard Heydrich, had to be expected. If this did nothing to help Joseph Schreieder sleep well, that too was unavoidable, and meanwhile the air-drops continued. Seventy-five wireless transmitters literally fell into German hands, along with three thousand Bren-guns, thousands of grenades, knives, flashlights and medical kits, tons of ammunition, Sten-guns by the thousands, bicycles, spare parts, a fortune in money, guilders, pounds sterling, francs and dollars. There was also clothing, tobacco, coffee, tinned food, even chocolate. Special warehouses were requisitioned, and a small army of clerks had to be assigned to inventory and guard it all.

Nor was that all. An even dozen US and British heavy bombers were shot down, either by anti-aircraft batteries or by Luftwaffe night fighters, and SOE continued to send great cannisters of supplies and agents. Sturmbannführer Schreieder noted that '. . . instructions from London [kept] . . . pouring in. Sergeant May and Sonderführer [Special Leader, a quasi-military rank] Huntemann worked seven days a week to de-code the messages; we had to compose replies and reports of imaginary sabotage activities . . . the signals had to be put in the SOE code . . . and all this meant hard work – particularly as we had to be careful to compose the message in phrases which the individual captured agents were likely to use.'

By the last week of November 1942, with the capture of agents George Russel and Johann de Kryuff, Giskes and Schreieder had fourteen captured wireless sets available for communication with London.

Perhaps inevitably Giskes' success aroused the ambition of others. Sonderführer Richard Christmann, one of Giskes' best counter-intelligence field men, the Abwehr agent who had accompanied Sergeant Karl Boden during the impersonation episode in France which had resulted in the destruction of the SOE 'Prosper' network, had excellent contacts in both Holland and Belgium. Through George Ridderhof he made the acquaintance of Resistance men involved with underground escape organizations, and during the course of establishing his own (bogus) escape route, he penetrated several Belgian Resistance groups, which he and Ridderhof delivered to the Germans. They did such a good job at this that they very nearly duplicated Herman Giskes' work in Holland. All but two or three of the Belgian networks were destroyed. But Christmann's ambition was to gain recognition from SOE as a specialist in his own right. And he succeeded.

By copying Giskes' system, he used several captured Belgian wireless posts to establish contact with both the SOE in London and the Belgian Ministry of Defence, which was part of the Belgian government in exile. By posing as the organizer and leader of an escape route for downed Allied airmen, secret agents and other fugitives, Christmann managed to extort a considerable amount of money from SOE. He also fabricated feats of sabotage and heroism. Under the name 'Richard Cholet', he invented a dramatic record of exploits which SOE swallowed hook, line and sinker. He was assigned the codename 'Arnaud', and by the time Herman Giskes ordered Christmann to stop his charade, SOE had invited him to Britain.

SOE also put Christmann up for a gallantry decoration, the Military Cross, with the approval of the War Office.

One of Christmann's stage-managed exploits was the 'escape' of four British secret agents, who were in fact members of the German military police.

One of these agents was 'arrested' *en route*. The remaining three were 'arrested' at a hotel in an elaborate raid in broad daylight complete with squads of military police surrounding the hotel and closing off several roads. It was made certain that newsmen were present when the trio of 'Resistance terrorists' were brought forth.

The newspaper coverage substantiated Christmann's allegation that his courageous attempt to help four Allied spies escape had been genuine. Herman Giskes helped Christmann win his Military Cross by radioing to London the details of this spectacular endeavour.

But Christmann never received his medal. When SOE wanted Christmann to visit London for the presentation, he made one excuse after another. (After the war Christmann duped the Americans into believing he had been a British Intelligence officer, but by that time the British were hard on his trail. When they caught up with him, Christmann resisted arrest and was shot dead.)

Events elsewhere by this time – the end of 1942 and the beginning of 1943 – were having an effect upon the war of the secret services. America was in the war with a vengeance. Combined United States–United Kingdom strength had the Germans in retreat in Africa. In the East, at Stalingrad, the *Untermensch* (subhumans) had given Germany her worst defeat since Jena, forcing Field Marshal Friedrich von Paulus to surrender all that remained of his great army, 24 generals, 2,000 officers, 90,000 ragged survivors, and on the ground, 175,000 dead or wounded. This event, concluded on 2 February 1943, augmented the creeping gloom which had for months been colouring every aspect of thought and conduct of all Germans.

In the conquered nations sabotage and subversion were increasing, along with daylight attacks upon German troops. There was defection and desertion. On the home front production was hindered by aerial attacks the Luftwaffe could not prevent. At sea the savage battle of the Atlantic, in which a fleet of German undersea vessels had been dominant for so long, was at long last beginning to favour the Allies, and above all there was little doubt but that an invasion of the Continent was coming. The fact that it did not occur for more than a year provided all those months for the psychological anxiety to do its work.

Among the Abwehr's directors, where perhaps five or six per cent of the total organization had been consistently anti-Nazi, the handwriting on the wall became clearer as time passed. Regardless of Tirpitzufer's efforts to influence the generals to seize Hitler, to make greater attempts to end the war, nothing was going to happen. When the Führer went down, Germany was going down with him. Nor could the Canaris clique do more than it had already done to reach an accord with the enemy, whose intransigence from the beginning had not wavered, although at times it had seemed that it might. The British were absolutely committed to one course and would not abandon it. Germany was not only going to be defeated, she was going to be made to pay in blood and stone for devastated London and obliterated Coventry and for all those dead and maimed – 625,791 of them yet to fall on the march to Berlin.

In Holland the same winds of change were blowing. The Abwehr and Sicherheitsdienst got their nineteenth radio link with London through the destruction of a network known as the 'National Committee', but victory in the Low Countries meant little without corresponding triumphs in Africa and Russia. Major Giskes – now a Lieutenant-Colonel – could continue to win his secret war until Allied troops knocked on the door of his 'Citadel'. But before anything that drastic occurred, a number of internees escaped from German custody, and every one of them had been serving underground radio posts which the Abwehr and SD had taken over. They knew the truth about the *England Spiel*.

Desperate efforts were made to recapture them, but as the weeks and months passed and the fugitives remained free, Herman Giskes became convinced 'that the bottom had been knocked out of the whole *England Spiel*. Even if the fugitives did not succeed in reaching Switzerland or Spain, they would report their experiences to some Resistance men and the report would somehow cross the Channel.'

He was correct, although it would be quite a while before it got to London. Eventually though, when SOE messages ceased to instruct and inform, and began to turn garrulous and innocuous, Hermann Giskes knew the masquerade was over and with condescending sarcasm sent his final message. This was in the spring of 1944. '. . . You are trying to make business in the Netherlands without our assistance . . . We think this rather unfair in view of our long and successful co-operation as your sole agents . . . But never mind, whenever you will come to pay a visit on the Continent you may be assured that you will be received with [the] same care and the result as [were] all those you sent us before . . . . So long.'

The *England Spiel* could not have continued much longer in any event. By 1944 not only was the war winding down for the Germans in all areas, but because aerial and naval superiority was now completely with the Allies, it was possible to infiltrate spies, saboteurs, arms and supplies in such enormous numbers and amounts that *Festung Europa* was beginning to appear as one vast territory upon the verge of a populist uprising.

Like a dagger in the back, *dénouement* also came from another direction. In Berlin, by this time, the enmity between the SD and the Abwehr was at the point where any plausible excuse for it to become openly pronounced would invoke a test of strength the Abwehr could not win. Admiral Canaris was the Chief of Military Intelligence, a department of defence, but the SD's chieftain, Heinrich Himmler, after Goering and Hitler, was number three in line of leadership of the entire nation.

The escape of those Dutch Resistance agents was all the SD needed to accuse the Abwehr of inefficiency, and Himmler, with the rank, power and authority, removed Giskes' *England Spiel* organization from Abwehr control and transferred it to SS Sturmbannführer Kienhardt's Funküberwachung (radio surveillance) department of the Gestapo. All this actually accomplished was to authorize Kienhardt to preside over the demise of one of the most spectacularly successful Intelligence operations of the war, one which kept a nation totally subjugated, compelled a cancellation of plans by the Allied Chiefs of Staff, and proved that German counter-intelligence was easily equal, if not superior, to its opposition. A post-war Dutch Parliamentary Commission called it 'A catastrophe which assumed proportions far in excess of any failure in any of the other German-occupied countries of Western Europe'. Subsequent historians were to say that the Abwehr's *coup* in Holland delayed the liberation of the Low Countries by months.

Those were the charitable writers. Others maintained that the Dutch people survived in spite of their German oppressors *and* their British friends.

(Giskes and Schreieder were taken into custody after the war and were investigated and interrogated by both Dutch and Allied prosecutors, as were a host of V-men including Antonius van der Waals. Neither Giskes nor Schreieder was charged; both were released. But van der Waals was sentenced in 1948 by a Dutch court and was put to death.)

What emerged into clear focus about the time Heinrich Himmler transferred the *England Spiel* to the SD, and before, was the competitive antagonism between Himmler's RSHA and the Abwehr. Reinhard Heydrich had not been the only member of the Reich Security Head Office who viewed the Abwehr with doubt, but at the field level, as in the instance of the co-operation between Joseph Schreieder and Herman Giskes, while the higher-echelon antipathy filtered down, there was little opportunity, even had the desire been prevalent, for the friction to create open hostility. At the operational level Abwehr and SD responsibilities were almost exclusively concerned with waging the counter-intelligence war. At the directory level it was the custom to pass directives for procedural implementation down to those whose purpose was to carry them out, which left ample time at the top for the political in-fighting which had begun before the war and did not stop until the war ended.

Men such as Herman Giskes and Joseph Schreieder did not know how serious the breach was at the top. They knew of the jealousy and the antagonism, but they had no idea there was treasonous subterfuge and intrigue at the top.

15

Unveiling the Colossus

The beginning of the Abwehr's decline could have been attributed to Admiral Canaris's estimate of two hundred combat-ready Soviet divisions, but in fact nothing in any war of great magnitude was ever that simple, even though it might seem to be.

After the war General Franz Halder, who served in Russia, said the Canaris estimate was grossly incorrect: '. . . the figure was more like three hundred and sixty [divisions].'

The Canaris figure was correct. The fault lay not with the Abwehr's estimate but with its ignorance of Soviet mobilization competence. At no time during the Russian campaign did the German army face only the Soviet army.

The Osoaviakhim, for example, was a nationwide paramilitary organization with regional cadres. It had 36 million members (of which thirty per cent were women) trained as part-time partisans. It was a home-guard variety of organization whose specialities were unorthodox warfare, harassment, night attacks and guerrilla activities. It could be, and was, mobilized on a moment's notice. Its members, sketchily armed, were loaded aboard convoys without front-line training, taken to combat areas, dumped out and sent headlong against the superbly disciplined veterans of the Wehrmacht, with appalling results. The Osoaviakhim increased Canaris's estimate of two hundred divisions to Halder's figure without their actually being part of the Soviet army.

The entire nation was subject to conscription. Factories, farms, offices were emptied without regard to age or limiting disabilities. NKVD machine-gun squads brought up the rear to prevent 'unauthorized withdrawals'. The NKVD, after which was patterned Himmler's RSHA, was the People's Commissariat of Internal Affairs. Throughout the war it was kept busy shooting deserters, stragglers, those separated from their combat units, and anyone suspected of collaboration or defeatism.

German Military Intelligence's blind spot was in limiting itself to counting only the divisions of the regular Soviet Army, and while this was its purpose – it was not an institution for the study of political or social structuring – the omission in this case was to prove disastrous.

However, although the blame fell on the Abwehr, with assistance from Heinrich Himmler, the actual fault lay elsewhere.

German Intelligence services had been accumulating information about Soviet war-making capabilities for twenty years through many sources including the various 'diplomatic corps'. In that length of time it should have done much better than it did. And yet, had the truth been available, Hitler's statement to von Rundstedt that 'you have only to kick in the door and the whole rotten structure will come down' epitomized German intransigence. And Hitler was wrong. The Osoaviakhim was a rarity, a very competent, highly motivated bureaucracy. Nor was it the only Soviet 'home guard'. There was also the Opolchenye, or 'People's Army', a genuine pastiche of weekend trainees who were never properly armed; they were frequently sent into battle with shotguns, a few bags of grenades, and bottles filled with gasoline. The best Opolchenye units, called 'Guards', were better outfitted, but by and large the 'People's Army' was simply a great horde of human beings, hundreds of thousands of them.

Finally there were the Party Battalions, from the Komosmol (Young Communist League) and the NKVD. These constituted a conglomeration of 'destruction battalions' created to fight as guerrillas. They were particularly trained to eliminate German parachutists and Russian defectors, of whom there were thousands. These Party Battalions also numbered into the hundreds of thousands. At the Battle of Leningrad, for example, a million of them worked round the clock to erect a series of earth and rubble defences encircling the city, then took part in the fighting.

The Germans learned early that they were facing situations inside Russia entirely different from those they had encountered in Europe. The resistance was not underground; it was openly above ground. A Soviet riposte had no subtlety, only head-long force, and Military Intelligence, for whatever reasons, had erred badly, if not in the circumstance of the combat-ready divisions, then elsewhere. For example, maps which were supplied to German units and which were drawn from information derived from Abwehr sources, were misleading. Field Marshal von Kluge's Chief of Staff, General Günther Blumentritt, said, 'We were not prepared for what we found because our maps in no way corresponded to reality . . . On our maps all supposed main roads were marked in red, and there seemed to be many, but they often proved to be merely sand tracks.'

Still, the opening stages of the Russian campaign were spectacularly successful. Hitler was in a jubilant mood even if his generals, who took the long view, were not. The full force of Russian resistance, including those rag-tag hordes of home guards, would not be able to make a dent in the superb Panzergruppen for months.

The Germans plunged with full confidence into a Soviet labyrinth occupied by millions of sacrificial Untermenschen, and rolled up victory after victory while their opponents struggled to piece together order from chaos, on the one hand, and yielded space for time on the other hand, more fortunate in this respect than the Europeans had been, because at least the Soviets had space to trade.

Hitler was again engaged on a grand scale. He was not the military blunderer he would be called later. He was in fact an excellent strategist; if, in reverse, he had possessed Russia's resources, he would have conquered Europe – and Germany. He was at his best when great forces were involved. The Russian campaign was the greatest land battle ever fought, and Hitler was its protagonist.

Nor did it sit well that there was opposition among the generals, and at least one admiral. Canaris had opposed *Barbarossa* from its inception. During the planning stages at Führerhauptquartier in the forest of Gorlitz not far from Rastenburg in East Prussia, Canaris's attitude contrasted directly with Hitler's confidence. Assuming, he said, Russia's strength at her borders was no better than Intelligence reports indicated, or even that beyond those borders she was poorly defended, the real question evolved around the conceivable reserves of a nation of approximately 180 million people.

How many divisions might the Soviets be able to raise if the Führer's timetable of a three to six months campaign should become twice or three times as long? Germany was at her absolute peak in manpower and production. No one had any idea what the Russian industrial capability was. Germany was producing 3,250 tanks annually (the sources vary). Up until now no one else had come close to that figure, but supposing the Russians could top it? Germany could not. (Halder said later the Russians produced 700 tanks a month – 8,400 annually – more than twice the German figure. But no one would have believed that possible in 1941–2, probably not even Admiral Canaris, who was reaching for any argument to scuttle *Barbarossa*.)

Canaris also brought up the bugaboo every Staff Officer had been stopped by since November 1812, the fearful Russian winter. He did something he had never done before and was never to do again: he spoke out directly in contradictory terms to Hitler. He might just as well have addressed the chandelier, except that the chandelier had no memory and Hitler had. He said Hitler's advisers were foolish and irresponsible. He would not be a party to this '. . . and could not understand how the generals, von Brauchitsch, Halder, Keitel and Jodl could be so . . . unrealistic, and so optimistic'.

It was useless. It was also dangerous. Wilhelm Keitel, senior member of the toady twins Keitel and Jodl, told the Admiral, 'My dear Canaris, you may have some understanding of Military Intelligence, but . . . you should not try to give us lessons in strategic and political planning.'

Hitler and his generals could afford to be tolerant because until the winter of 1941–2 the Abwehr had acquitted itself well. Giskes' excellent showing in the Low Countries was one of many Abwehr successes. Hugo Bleicher, Heinz Eckert and other Intelligence personnel had crushed the major SOE-supported Resistance networks in France. Even in the peripheral areas of Greece and Turkey, the Intelligence communities were easily the match of all opposition, but nonetheless Canaris's criticism had not set well, and an unrelated event during the last week of February 1942 brought forth Hitler's wrath. Aside from his smouldering resentment of the Admiral's candour, this event aggravated the Führer in an area where he was especially sensitive. He had always reacted harshly to unorthodox conflict, even though no one approved of it more than he did when Germans engaged in it.

In the last week of February 1942 British paratroops raided the special German radar post near Le Havre at Bruneval, which contained top secret Würzburg detection equipment. This commando-style attack consisted of two elements: specialists trained to dismantle the equipment, and an armed force to engage the German detachment of guards. It was a success. The equipment was carried down a six-hundred-foot cliff to waiting boats, which sped across the Channel where Allied electronics experts were waiting. The purpose of this raid was to provide Allied experts with an opportunity to study German radar so that effective counter-measures could be developed.

Hitler flew into a rage. Commando attacks invariably had this effect on him, and of late they had been increasing. They were usually swift, totally unexpected, murderous, demoralizing, and although the number of Germans slain was small, the manner in which they were killed was in Hitler's opinion completely criminal. He may have been correct: commandos killed by knife thrusts in the back, by strangulation and by silencered handguns, gangster methods to be sure; but Hitler's indignation was bizarre: *he* killed by gas-chamber, poison injection and *Genichschuss*.

How was it, he wanted to know, that the British Secret Services could accomplish these attacks while the German Secret Services could not? What, he demanded of Admiral Canaris, had the Abwehr done with its own stealth and mayhem unit, the Brandenburgers? Where were the Abwehr files on British counter-measure Intelligence?

Canaris had almost nothing on enemy electronic espionage. Nor had he been able to plant agents in Britain who could work up anything on the very secret commando units, which were never large or susceptible to penetration. Nor was Hitler's comparison of the British commandos and the Brandenburger regiments quite apt.

Nonetheless the Führer sent for Heinrich Himmler. He had been alienated twice, first by what he was convinced was an

Abwehr blunder in the matter of those two hundred Soviet divisions, and more recently by Canaris's excoriation of the Russian invasion. He decreed that henceforth the SD would be responsible for gathering information concerning British counter-intelligence.

For Military Intelligence this was the first in a series of detractions which were to undermine the Abwehr. For Admiral Canaris it was a defeat in his struggle to maintain autonomy for Abwehr counter-intelligence, but in fact the loss of confidence was not exclusive with Hitler. Among the officers of the OKW, scepticism had been surfacing since the slaying of Reinhard Heydrich by assassins found to have British Army paybooks. If German counter-intelligence could not prevent this sort of thing, then every German officer was in danger, even those of the Oberkommando der Wehrmacht.

The Generals were wary because of something else. They were cognizant of the plotting against Hitler, and although not one of them had picked up a telephone to call Himmler, most of them knew there was Abwehr culpability. No one in the intrigue-ridden Nazi hierarchy would be foolish enough not to disassociate himself from an organization whose favour was declining and whose future was uncertain.

As for Hitler's comparison between British commandos and the Brandenburgers, what made them basically different was that Britain between 1941 and 1942 was defensive, and for these same years Germany was offensive.

As in the affair of the Bruneval radar post, British commando strikes were swift, limited and rarely prolonged. They could count on no armed support from local troops. The Brandenburgers on the other hand (so-called because their training and supply facility was at Brandenburg, forty miles west of Berlin) were uniformed volunteers for special services who served with, and were supported by, the armed forces.

Formed in 1939 as the Brandenburg Training Company, it served under Division II (von Lahousen: sabotage and special duties) of the Abwehr. Composed mainly of Balts and *Volksdeutschen* (foreign nationals of German descent who spoke German), it was commanded by Lieutenant-Colonel Heinz, who was a confidant of Canaris, von Lahousen and Oster. He was also party to the various schemes to overthrow Hitler.

Brandenburgers engaged in all manner of clandestine activities behind enemy lines, but they operated as part of the combat armies, often in enemy uniforms. The SD, especially Heydrich in his day, opposed the idea of the Abwehr controlling troops of any kind. But in fact, because Brandenburgers were fanatically loyal Nazis (otherwise they would not have volunteered to serve in an outfit which consistently put them into situations where capture meant execution), it was very improbably that they would have obeyed orders inimical to the Nazi regime.

But in any event, while they performed commando-type deeds, they did so to further Wehrmacht objectives. For example, in 1940 Brandenburg volunteers of a special force (Z.b.V: *Zur besondern Verwendung*, 'for special utilization') dressed in uniforms of the Belgian Army and secured the bridges at Gennep so that the advancing German 6th Army could maintain its invasion timetable; again, in Romania, Brandenburgers thwarted Allied efforts to destroy Romanian oilfields by already being on hand as clerks, watchmen and administrative and field personnel.

Generally Brandenburgers, while nominally controlled by Abwehr II, were under the command of corps area commanders and their ICs, or General Staff officers in a combat area who were responsible for Intelligence work.

What this amounted to was that, while the Abwehr was responsible for the technical maintenance, tactical orders came from the Wehrmacht commanders in the field. Similarly, while the SS was largely autonomous too, separate from the Regular Army, in combat theatres orders to the SS came from tactical officers. In both cases it was not a very efficient or happy arrangement, but nothing better was ever devised. However, when Hitler railed at Canaris after the Bruneval raid, his mention of the Brandenburgers was not appropriate. He would have demonstrated a more thorough knowledge had he simply said commandos, because the Germans had commando units which operated in exactly the same fashion as did British commandos, but in a rage Hitler was never entirely rational, nor for that matter was he entirely lucid, and in this instance his anger towards Admiral Canaris and the Abwehr was, as Walter Schellenberg noted, the beginning of the end.

But only a few months earlier an episode occurred in which Canaris's hand was spectrally discernible and which would have solved most of the problems for the Army as well as the Abwehr. The arrest of Adolf Hitler, if it had succeeded.

It occurred in the summer of 1941, when the armies in Russia were triumphant, strung out and in one of their frequent periods of indecision and dispute.

Heinz Guderian, the great tank general, an individual whose prescience probably entitled him to be a *prima donna* among field officers, had never yielded in his conviction that the key to victory was Moscow. In a series of swashbuckling victories he had cleared a path in that direction for Army Group Centre, Field Marshal Fedor von Bock's command, although Hitler had earlier decreed that the destruction of the Russian armies, not the fall of their capital, was the German objective.

Guderian's superiors, von Bock and Halder, unable to approve although each was tacitly in agreement, put it up to von Brauchitsch, who approved and put the argument in memorandum form to Hitler.

The Führer's reaction was predictable. He sent forth Directive 34 in which it was stated that German objectives were the Crimea, the Donetz Basin and the occupation of Russia's Caucasian oilfields, not Moscow.

Halder grumbled, which he did often; von Bock was disappointed – he envisioned himself as an historical individual, the Captor of Moscow – but Heinz Guderian considered resigning from the army, and von Brauchitsch, a seasoned straddler of fences, sought to salvage the situation through a conference at Novy Borisov, von Bock's headquarters, and to everyone's surprise Hitler agreed to attend. It would be the first time he had entered Russia since the campaign began.

Naturally there was great anxiety. It was not to be a tour of inspection, and those to attend were familiar with Hitler's sudden, dramatic rages. To heighten the anxiety, '. . . the headquarters of Army Group Centre had become "the immediate centre of active operational conspiracy – a nest of intrigue and treason" . . . which affected every member of the staff'.

Bock's GSO IC (General Staff Officer, Intelligence command) was Major-General Henning von Tresckow. His aide was Major Fabian von Schlabrendorff, the same officer who, on instructions from Abwehr Central Section's Hans Oster, had visited the British diplomatic mission at the Hotel Adlon the day war came in 1939, to inform the British military attaché, Colonel Dennis Daley, that the opposition to Hitler would attempt to open an avenue of communication with the British government through the Vatican. Both von Tresckow and Fabian von Schlabrendorff had been conspirators against Hitler since those early days.

Tresckow's duty as IC was to interpret for the Commanding General – von Bock – Intelligence information supplied by the Abwehr. It had always been Canaris's policy to promote goodwill between the GSO ICs and Military Intelligence. Fabian von Schlabrendorff was not only von Tresckow's aide, he was also the Abwehr's liaison officer with Army Group Centre. They were close collaborators, and when Hitler's attendance at the Novy Borisov meeting was confirmed, von Tresckow and von Schlabrendorff saw this as an opportunity which probably would not come again. They accordingly worked out a scheme of abduction which was remarkably naïve in its simplicity and which, under the circumstances which obtained in the euphoric summer of 1941, undoubtedly would have resulted in their execution. As von Brauchitsch had once said, simply removing Hitler would not be enough. Nonetheless, von Tresckow and von Schlabrendorff persevered.

Brought into the conspiracy were von Bock's two aides, Graf Heinrich von Lehndorff and Graf Hans von Hardenberg. Very probably von Bock himself had an inkling. He was certainly not '*führertreu*', and later he would be swayed. He had to realize there was an increasing groundswell of opposition to Hitler.

Others who became involved were Colonel Freiherr von Gersdorff, Lieutenant-Colonel Alexander von Voss, Colonel Schultz-Buttger and all of von Bock's staff, as well as a number of minor officers.

The actual abduction was to take place when Hitler's entourage entered the area of Army Group Centre's security grid, where the plotters had jurisdiction. Hitler's car was to be diverted, its occupant arrested, detained and subjected to a trial with the foregone verdict to be his removal as leader of the nation or, and this appears not to have been generally discussed, sentenced to death and executed.

It was at best an extremely hazardous enterprise. There were strong SS commands in the area. The SS was, originally at any rate, indoctrinated with fanatical loyalty to the Führer. If von Bock had taken a stand favouring the conspirators, which was no certainty at all, he could conceivably have used the Regular Army to disarm the SS. But an internecine struggle among the Germans, with Russian armies converging on them, would hardly have appealed to as seasoned a soldier as von Bock.

Then the siege of nerves began. Hitler's personal security officers were anything but naïve. They knew the Führer was a prime target for half the world's conspirators. Three times it was announced Hitler would embark from the Führerhauptquartier near Rastenburg, and three times he did not leave, but his security officers made exploratory excursions. Finally, on 3 August, carloads of SS arrived to secure the area, in conjunction with von Bock's security officers – who were the plotters.

Hitler's aeroplane landed three miles from headquarters and was met by SS detachment. The cars lined out one behind the other for the return trip. Because security ordained that Hitler was never to ride twice in the same vehicle in situations of this kind, the waiting conspirators were unable to discern which car he was in, and when the long, dusty convoy entered von Bock's security area, they were at a loss.

At headquarters, where Hitler took over von Bock's map-room, security was so tight that the conspirators were thwarted again. SS guards were at the map-room door and outside on patrol, and inside was General Rudolf Schmundt, Hitler's army adjutant, and more SS.

While the conspirators procrastinated, Hitler interviewed the Generals separately, then called them together and declared that Leningrad was to be their objective: after it fell, he would decide whether the Ukraine or Moscow would be next, his preference, for strategic and economic reasons, being the Ukraine. Then he left Novy Borisov as he had reached it, unscathed, and for half a month afterwards the officers he had left behind, not only the conspirators but also von Bock and Guderian, functioned in a pall of gloom, their pet project,

Moscow, only 150 miles due east, saved from attack for the time being.

But Hitler had not been entirely uninfluenced. 'While flying back,' he wrote, 'I decided in any case to make the necessary preparations for an attack on Moscow.'

What really came out of the Novy Borisov meeting was delay, and in a fluid battlefield situation such as the Wehrmacht faced that summer, procrastination was by far the greater enemy. The priceless days of summer, which meant dry roadbeds and agreeable temperatures, were slipping past. Soon the ghosts of Bonaparte would be present in the crisp, clear, star-bright nights.

16

Towards Cannae

Until the invasion of Russia, nothing in the history of the nation or the career of its Führer had inherent in its undertaking such horror for both, and as the 'six months campaign' moved from triumph to triumph without an end in sight, the cold grip of fear was tinged with an incredible irony: Hitler and Germany could be absolutely destroyed by all those victories.

Understandably, his attention was riveted eastward. He had assumed total command. All the Army Group generals such as Rundstedt and Stuelpnagel had been dismissed or retired. Hitler's commitment was eastward, and in other areas of concern there ensued a variety of procrastination which throve on indecision.

In the Balkans, Italy and Africa, problems were crystallizing which local Germans recognized but lacked the authority to redress, and no one particularly cared to bring these things to Hitler's attention. The ancient Greeks were not the only people who upon occasion destroyed messengers bearing ill tidings.

The victories continued: a war of movement favoured the Germans right up until the moment von Paulus entered Stalingrad, Rommel was checkmated at El Alamein, and Montgomery launched his *Lightfoot* offensive which caught the Germans by surprise, and meanwhile the strain on German Military Intelligence increased hourly. Each theatre required the best Intelligence possible in the least time.

Tirpitzufer's lights blazed throughout the night; messengers, cryptologists and code machines got no rest. It was imperative that the Canaris organization support the nation in its most critical time, while the Schwarze Kapelle's conspirators, including Canaris, simultaneously plotted against the individual who had brought calamity to the nation. The ambiguity of serving Germany but not its Führer created insoluble problems. For the Abwehr the years of stress were leading Military Intelligence down a direct road to *dénouement*.

Abwehr Intelligence analyses had become suspect. The open secret of Canaris's duplicity, of his shadow leadership of the anti-Nazi Schwarze Kapelle, of Hitler's increasing disenchantment with Military Intelligence, undermined Abwehr credibility.

Then came *Torch*, the Allied sea-going activity in Atlantic waters which the Kriegsmarine, not Military Intelligence, uncovered. None of the legerdemain of high Intelligence or sophisticated counter-intelligence dramatically revealed how the ships which had been under surveillance for so long had suddenly rendezvoused, although the actual accumulation of transports had not gone unnoticed, and it was assumed that, when the transports were loaded, they might set course for Dakar in French West Africa.

The Navy had aligned a screen of forty U-boats between Gibraltar and Dakar, but everyone operated on assumption. German Intelligence knew less than submarine ratings who raised and lowered periscopes for visual contact.

Then the rendezvous took place, the *Torch* armada sailed and Hitler was *en route* to Munich in his private train for the annual celebration of the 1923 Beer Hall *Putsch* when teleprinter reports informed him that a vast flotilla of Allied ships had steamed through the Strait of Gibraltar into the Mediterranean, and at long last an event outside Russia caught the Führer's attention. He demanded full details from Intelligence sources, but no one, including Admiral Canaris, had anything to report, and in their eagerness to come up with something, Germany's best brains in the field of deception were themselves deceived, not once but twice.

Torch was an Allied initiative. Deception networks including the XX Committee and Churchill's brainchild, the London Controlling Section (LCS), co-ordinated an incredible ruse, one of the most successful of the war. What the Abwehr pieced together was that an Allied force planned to invade Africa from a staging area at Dakar. Hitler and his generals accepted this without suspecting it was a deliberate deception which had been fed to German Intelligence. The second phase of the deception resolved the peril inherent in the U-boat screen. The Kriegsmarine was informed through Abwehr channels that a second armada was outward bound from Sierra Leone for Britain. Again, this information was fed into the German counter-Intelligence system at a time when desperate German Intelligence agencies were grasping at straws. Orders went forth for the second fleet, known as Convoy SL125, to be destroyed, and accordingly the U-boat screen went in pursuit.

Convoy SL125, under the command of Rear-Admiral E. N. Reyne, consisted of empty cargo vessels. The hit-and-run battle which ensued cost Convoy SL125 thirteen ships during a week-long engagement of hide-and-seek, while elsewhere the great *Torch* fleet sailed toward the coast of Africa. But at Dakar, where an assault was anticipated, nothing happened, and the passage of time heightened the mystery.

Alfred Jodl was of the opinion, based on 'somewhat vague reports . . . that the Anglo-Saxons intend multiple landings in West Africa', but he also wondered if the landing might not occur at Malta. Finally, starved for Intelligence, Jodl made an ominous judgement even before the Allied fleet reached its destination, when he said, 'Once again Canaris has let us down through his irrationality and instability.'

What had so effectively kept the Germans in the dark was the Allied ban on radio communication in all areas excepting those concerned with deception. The great *Torch* fleet was disembarking troops and equipment upon a vast line from Casablanca past Oran to Bougie before German Intelligence was able to sift through the prevarication and discover the truth.

Hitler was aroused from bed at two o'clock in the morning to read the reports, and more than a year later he would reflect upon the surprises he felt that night by saying, 'We didn't even dream of it.'

He was not alone. From Jodl's suspicion that Malta might be the target, to other conjectures ranging from an Allied landing in Sicily, or the coast of central Italy, even the southern shoreline of France, those who thought the assault would occur in Africa did not expect it to take place in French North-west Africa.

This Allied success guaranteed the loss of Africa. It also put an Allied force within striking distance of Mussolini's Fascist homeland. It lay as a shadow of menace across a part of Hitler's domain which until that time had been secure.

How badly had German Intelligence failed? The *Torch* fleet consisted of more than 1,500 ships, 90,000 men (later, another 200,000) all their supplies, ammunition and rolling stock. It was at that time the greatest invasion fleet ever assembled. No Intelligence failure in history could match this one, and nothing Hitler could do, including an ensuing reshuffling of his African and Mediterranean forces, could fundamentally alter the situation.

(There was a footnote to the *Torch* episode which was not revealed until after the war. Admiral Canaris's station chief at Hamburg, Captain Herman Wichman, did in fact discover the destination of the *Torch* fleet. He sent this information by special messenger to the OKW by way of Tirpitzufer. It was never received by the OKW.)

At this juncture the war in the East was approaching a terrible climax. Hitler's anxieties over conditions in Africa and Mediterrania were superseded by such blood-lettings as Leningrad and Stalingrad, the latter an unparalleled disaster for German arms, the former a harrowing example of what was required of civilians alone to stop a German juggernaut; during the siege 35,000 of them starved to death.

Elsewhere, while dissatisfaction with Admiral Canaris and the Abwehr was increasing along the corridors of power, a widespread pall of gloom was spreading over the nation, and that intransigent old oppositionist Ludwig Beck, seemingly unmindful of his personal peril, was still aggravating the consciences of former comrades. He told Canaris that now, finally, German officers would actively support a conspiracy against Hitler. According to Ludwig Beck, the hour of the Schwarze Kapelle had arrived, and indeed there would not be a second opportunity to save the nation.

He may not have realized how accurate his prediction was. Those troubled procrastinators of high rank no longer comprised a majority of the membership. The Schwarze Kapelle did not now exist as an ultra-secret fraternity of generals and field marshals who realized what must be done but lacked the courage to do it. Nor was it any longer a closet group operating

in such extreme secrecy that it lacked substance and organization, and yet not all those who were shortly to oppose the
Führer actively were members. Defeat in the East and West
brought with it a widespread realization that total catastrophe
was imminent. Common soldiers, non-commissioned officers,
junior rankers, dozen of civilian industrialists who served the
munition, transportation, weapons, even medical and clothing
requirements of the armed services, saw clearly that as long as
Hitler was supreme there was no hope. These people required
direction; at the very least some idea that others like themselves were willing to take action. When the decision was
eventually reached to kill Hitler, even though the actual
planning was a Schwarze Kapelle undertaking, dozens of
non-members gave solid support. And this time, by utilizing
conduits of communication from Tirpitzufer to Paris in the
West and Smolensk in the East, a carefully orchestrated but
tenuously complicated plan was conceived.

If, in retrospect, it would appear that Operation *Flash*, as the
assassination scheme was called, was needlessly circuitous,
that was understandable, because every intrigue its foremost
protagonist became involved with was tortuously circuitous.

Operation *Flash*, the plan for the actual killing of Hitler, was
linked to *Case Valkyrie*, a paralleling project by which the
conspirators proposed to seize power and administer the
country after Hitler's death, and again the shadowy eminence
of the paramount plotter, Admiral Canaris, was discernible.
Canaris had consistently avoided the simple, direct course of
raw violence, *Genichschuss*, for Hitler.

The *Valkyrie* concept was not new, although the Canaris
version was. Back in the spring of 1942 a *Plan Valkyrie* had
been drafted whereby in the event of internal disturbances
home units of the Wehrmacht would be mobilized to preserve
order.

The Schwarze Kapelle version proposed to use these troops
to protect and preserve the post-Hitler anti-Nazi government,
something which obviously had never been the intention of the
original *Valkyrie* planners.

The 'Home Army' to be used in the event of an emergency
inside Germany, would be under the command of the military
internal security chieftain, General Erich Fromm. The actual

details of how *Valkyrie* would function in an emergency were drawn up by Fromm's Chief-of-Staff, General Friedrich Olbricht, who was a member of the Schwarze Kapelle. It was Olbricht who recognized the value of a large Home Army to support rather than suppress a revolt against Hitler.

In the early summer of 1942, Admiral Canaris had directed Hitler's attention to a significant statistic: there were four million impressed foreigners working inside the country, and by 1944 Canaris's projection showed twice that many.

In the event of internal trouble, between four and eight million anti-German labourers could become a distinct threat to the nation. It was from this conceivable peril that Hitler's decree to form the Home Army had derived.

A second individual of authority, Production Minister Albert Speer, brought an additional reason to Hitler's attention for maintaining a strong Home Army. He feared a landing of Allied paraforces at the vital ports of Hamburg and Bremen through which beach-heads could be established to permit large invading armies to land from Allied fleets, in which case, he said, without adequate home defence forces, Berlin itself might be occupied 'within a few days'.

Alfred Jodl sarcastically referred to Speer, an architect by profession, as an 'armchair strategist', but Hitler was impressed. The result was that *Plan Valkyrie* assumed fresh significance for the Führer after the Allied North-west Africa venture became a fact.

What Friedrich Olbricht drafted into the *Valkyrie* plan was seemingly appropriate provisions which vested in General Fromm executive authority in the event Hitler was out of the country when an emergency arose. This would also provide Fromm with executive power in the event Hitler was dead.

Olbricht knew his Commander; General Fromm was not a member of the Schwarze Kapelle but neither was he Führer-treu. As a professional soldier, who also occasionally enjoyed not being one, Erich Fromm was a likeable, sturdy, shrewd man who had shared his private doubts with his friend and Chief-of-Staff. He was also a practical man; if Hitler were dead, Fromm would not hesitate to use executive power to maintain order. He and Friedrich Olbricht worked well together; each had implicit trust in the other. Fromm had authorized his Chief-of-Staff to sign orders and decrees in his name, and it was with this authority that Olbricht was able to assume for himself as Fromm's deputy the right to impose martial law, order summary executions, command all internal armed forces, even of the SS, and employ Home Army force to assure that his orders were obeyed.

The actual force of the Home Army was defined in Alfred Jodl's diary: 'Skeletal divisions are to be created in Germany into which in an emergency the men on leave and the convalescents can be pumped. Speer will provide weapons by a crash programme. There are always three hundred thousand men on furlough at home; that means ten or twelve divisions.'

A force that large, as well as a conspiracy as encompassing as *Flash-Valkyrie*, required a popular figurehead, and the man who was at that time a logical choice was Field Marshal Hans Guenther von Kluge, Commander-in-Chief before Moscow, a soldier's soldier in the George S. Patton mould but with better instincts. Kluge had led victorious German armies in Poland, had forced the Belgian army to surrender, had shattered the French at Rouen, had outmanoeuvred the British at Dunkirk, and in Russia had defeated every Soviet force sent against him. He was a popular hero at home and had the confidence of Adolf Hitler. He was also as nearly apolitical as a career soldier could be, and at sixty was unlikely to change, which made him less than an ideal individual to depend upon in a political crisis, but the optimists in the Schwarze Kapelle had some reason to be hopeful. One reason was that the same Major-General Henning von Tresckow who had served von Bock, and who had been a leader in the miscued assassination scheme at Novy Borisov, was von Kluge's Chief-of-Staff. With von Tresckow was another Schwarze Kapelle member of that earlier episode, Fabian von Schlabrendorff. Certainly von Tresckow had encouraged the plotters in Berlin to believe that von Kluge might be amenable.

Ludwig Beck particularly wanted von Kluge in the conspiracy. The Field Marshal's popularity with the Wehrmacht rank and file as well as the civilians at home would go far toward minimizing a backlash or counter-rebellion after Hitler was brought down.

At von Kluge's Army Group Centre headquarters near

Smolensk, Tresckow and Schlabrendorff sought diligently to influence the Field Marshal, and succeeded to the extent that von Kluge agreed to invite Hitler to visit him, but before that they induced the Field Marshal to receive a lean old anti-Nazi named Karl-Friedrich Goerdeler, at one time Oberbürgermeister at Leipzig and now one of Beck's and Canaris's most confirmed confederates.

At this meeting of totally divergent personalities, Goerdeler's forthrightness contrasted with von Kluge's ambiguity, but Goerdeler had nothing to lose while the Field Marshal, a national hero in the mould of the great Teutonic knights, had everything to lose. The upshot was that von Kluge said he could do nothing until Hitler was dead, but once that had been taken care of, he would align himself with the conspiracy. Goerdeler took this back to Berlin with him, and with military disasters in the making on all sides, von Kluge invited Hitler to Smolensk.

Hitler accepted, and the Tirpitzufer conspirators were immediately informed. Admiral Canaris made arrangements to visit Army Group Centre headquarters with his staff and department chiefs, ostensibly to convene an Intelligence conference, actually to deliver the components of a soundless time-bomb and to verify what Goerdeler had reported about von Kluge's willingness to join the conspiracy. He arrived a week before Hitler was due, which allowed ample time to perfect the details of the assassination. Before he left Berlin, General Olbricht had assured him that, the moment the code-word 'Flash' was received in Berlin, signifying success, that Hitler was dead, Olbricht would set in motion the machinery which would invoke the Home Army's executive authority. Elsewhere, other members of the Black Choir would be waiting, their functions ranging from contacting the Allied leadership for an immediate end of the fighting, to sealing Germany's borders and checkmating moves by the SS or Himmler's organization to assume national leadership.

Field Marshal von Kluge had a week of nervous stomach and diminishing resolve as he pretended not to know what Canaris and his associates were about.

Originally Hitler was to be shot by officers of the 24th Cavalry Regiment under the aegis of Lieutenant-Colonel

Freiherr von Boeselager, who would also overpower the Führer's SS bodyguard. The alternative method of dispatch was to be the time-bomb.

Obviously, if Hitler were shot to death at Army Group Centre headquarters, whatever history and the German people might think of that, von Kluge's reputation would sustain the identical odium which had accrued to Brutus. No German Knight could live with that, so von Kluge told von Tresckow there was to be no assassination at Smolensk. He did not, however, convey this decision until Admiral Canaris and his officers had enplaned for Berlin, in order to be in the capital when word of Hitler's death arrived.

Tresckow and Schlabrendorff proceeded then to their alternative murder method. For several days they experimented on a remote and unused Red Army firing range with the British-made explosive – from captured SOE stores – which Canaris's Section Chief, General Erwin von Lahousen, had brought to them. This consisted of sheets of nitro-tetramethanium which could be stacked together to create a bomb of whatever power was desired. The nitro-tetramethanium had three kinds of fuse, a ten-minute, a thirty-minute and a two-hour fuse. It was decided that the half-hour detonator should be used, and the camouflaged bomb would be placed on Hitler's aircraft when he was ready to leave Smolensk for the return to East Prussia.

At about midday on 13 March 1943 Hitler's Focke-Wulf-200 transport put down at Army Group Centre's landing strip, along with the customary escort of Me-109 fighter aircraft, and a second transport carrying Hitler's vegetarian cook, Fräulein Manziali, Dr Morell, Hitler's personal physician, and the hand-picked detail of twenty-five SS bodyguards. The Führer was taken at once to von Kluge's headquarters for a brief conference before lunch. Both von Tresckow and Major von Schlabrendorff were on hand. After lunch there was another conference, then Hitler was ready for the flight home.

General von Tresckow solicited a favour from Colonel Heinz Brandt of the entourage. Would it be possible for Brandt to take back to East Prussia with him a package containing two bottles of brandy for General Helmuth Stieff at Rastenburg? Colonel Brandt would be pleased to deliver the liquor. Tresckow and Schlabrendorff accompanied the entourage back to the landing strip, and at the last moment Major Schlabrendorff handed Colonel Brandt the package of 'brandy bottles'. Inside were the sheets of nitrotetramethanium. They had been wrapped below a vial of corrosive acid which, when broken, would eat through a wire restraining the detonator. The explosion would occur, according to von Tresckow's estimate, about the time Hitler's aircraft was over Minsk. As von Schlabrendorff handed Colonel Brandt the package, he exerted finger-pressure and broke the vial.

The officers returned to headquarters and waited. Major von Schlabrendorff called Berlin to report that the bomb was aboard Hitler's aeroplane. Then he and von Tresckow listened to radio reports for the announcement which never came. Three hours later a coded teletype message routinely informed Field Marshal von Kluge that the Führer had reached Rastenburg safely.

Schlabrendorff immediately contacted Berlin to say that the plan had failed. He had no idea how, but obviously and at great personal risk he had to find out. Tresckow called Colonel Brandt at Rastenburg to ask if the 'brandy' had been delivered to General Stieff. It had not, Brandt replied; the entourage had been too busy since returning, but . . . von Tresckow quickly said no, Colonel Brandt should keep the package; it was the wrong one. Major von Schlabrendorff would be in Rastenburg the following day on his way to Berlin and would bring the proper package.

The following morning von Schlabrendorff rode the regular courier aircraft to Rastenburg, retrieved the packaged bomb, left another package, this time actually containing two bottles of Cointreau, and engaged passage on a train leaving Korschen for Berlin. Locked inside a private compartment, von Schlabrendorff used a razor blade to open the package. As he wrote later: 'Having stripped the cover, I could see that both explosive charges were unaltered.' He removed the detonator. What he found, to his great surprise, was that, 'The fuse had worked; the glass globule had broken; the corrosive fluid had consumed the retainer wire; the striker had operated; but the detonator cap had not reacted.'

A subsequent chronicler of this event noted that, 'The

Devil's hand had protected Hitler.' Perhaps, but a more prosaic explanation seems equally reasonable. While Hitler's aeroplane was approaching Minsk, according to the pilot, considerable turbulence had been encountered. To spare Hitler unnecessary discomfort, the pilot had climbed well above the customary eight-thousand-feet level. The temperature in the luggage compartment of the aircraft dropped below freezing. Both the acid and the detonator had frozen. The detonator was ruined. After resuming flight at the normal altitude, while the acid thawed, the detonator would not function.

The *Flash-Valkyrie* conspiracy was dead. Disillusionment was widespread, and those in highest Allied Intelligence circles who had also been monitoring airwaves over Minsk, became convinced anew that none of the obviously sincere but clearly inept conspirators inside Germany was going to contribute to an early end to the war.

For Beck, Canaris, Tresckow, Schlabrendorff and dozens of other men in the Schwarze Kapelle, this latest failure did more than cause a climate of disillusionment; it also seriously, perhaps fatally, discredited their clandestine organization.

17

The Weaving Winds of War

Field Marshal von Kluge's nickname was 'Kluger Hans', 'Wily Jack', and he had lived up to it during conversations with Admiral Canaris at Smolensk before the débâcle of the inoperable nitrotetramethanium bomb. Whatever he had told Goerdeler, or whatever interpretation Goerdeler put on those remarks, von Kluge was less evasive with Canaris. He could not support an insurrection against Hitler, he said, while the nation's fate was in the military balance. A great, probably decisive, battle was shaping up in Russia. He could not divide his attention at this time.

It was the truth, but there was more to it than that. The Field Marshal had been challenged upon several occasions by Guderian, who had never accepted procrastination with good grace. Kluge had been static for months. Guderian, the invincible tanker, thought in terms of movement as opposed to von Kluge's caution and prolonged periods of what appeared to be indecision.

The von Kluge of Poland, Belgium and France, where movement never involved vast distances, and at a time when German resources and power were at their zenith, was a different man from von Kluge at Smolensk facing shortages, fearful of Russian distances and now aware that participation in a rebellion against Hitler could quite possibly cast him in von Paulus's role as another dishonoured hero. Instinctively he disassociated himself from the conspiracy, but he did so without actually slamming the door in case the conspiracy succeeded. 'Wily Jack's' ambivalence was bound to leave Admiral Canaris with a feeling of great disappointment, even betrayal, but von Kluge was not the only German general who had done that.

Yet in fairness, as long as von Kluge's position was as unenviable as it undeniably was, caught between the Russians and an insubordinate field commander, he had more than enough to worry about. Two months after the Smolensk conference his exasperation reached a point where he requested permission of Hitler to challenge Guderian to a duel.

For Canaris and the Schwarze Kapelle neither anything as ridiculous as a duel between German general officers, or the increasingly ominous cacophony of a blood-bath entering its most savagely contested phase, could quite obscure other developments.

Three months before the Admiral had visited Smolensk, the United States President, Franklin Delano Roosevelt, had called for Germany's 'unconditional surrender'. His British allies thought it a poor choice of words. So did Canaris, because now, with no alternative to fighting down to the last bullet, Germany would be as little susceptible to a rebellion from within as it would be to a dictated surrender from without.

Another development had to do with the Abwehr itself. After so many months of skating on the very thin ice of duplicity, there were reasons to believe that disaster through disclosure was not very distant. For several years Canaris's inner circle of confidants, Piekenbrock, Dohnanyi, Oster, von Lahousen, von Bentivegni, *et al.*, along with their sympathetic couriers, representatives and emissaries to the Vatican, to the various foreign embassies and to the Schwarze Kapelle, as well as the closet groups of other anti-Nazi elements which existed in other German Intelligence agencies, and in the armed forces, had been leaving unavoidable evidence of their connivance. The wonder is not that they were able so successfully to locate so many kindred spirits, but that they were able to do it so well for so long. But inevitably – and they all seemed to know this – the clandestine meetings in the rear seats of cars, at church doorways, in darkened hotel rooms, left trails, and in a nation whose internal security services had something like a quarter of a million informants and spies, every trail which was uncovered – and most were sooner or later – led to a conspiracy.

As the war approached its zenith in the East, the tempo of all things having a bearing on the nation's existence quickened. What three years earlier had taken half a year, or a full year, to conclude, by late 1943 had to be concluded in weeks and months; the great machine of men and equipment, which had bought time for Germany between 1939 and 1942, was swiftly reaching the point by late 1942 and 1943 where, even had spare parts for the tanks, field-guns and aircraft been available – and to some extent they were – the tanks and guns and aircraft no longer existed. Nor did the men. Spare parts, even new weapons and machines, could be brought to maturity in months; it required close to eighteen years to rear and train the men who would serve the tanks, guns and aircraft.

The quickening tempo was not entirely a result of battlefield or Intelligence difficulties. Germany's patchwork of political alliances, half of which were the result of nothing more lofty than expediency, was tearing out at the seams. Abwehr reports to the OKW, supported by embassy analyses from Hungary, Romania, Italy, Bulgaria, even Austria, left no doubt that the stunning losses, and the discernibility of unavoidable defeat, were hastening the dissolution. Two years earlier Italian officers told Hans von Dohnanyi, who was at that time Oster's Abwehr deputy chief of Central Section, that a conspiracy was afoot to overthrow Mussolini and take Italy out of the war by 1942. It did not happen, not in 1942, but by 1943, when the activists seemed likely to succeed and this information reached Berlin, Hitler threatened to invade Italy and simultaneously ordered an Intelligence penetration with a view to uncovering the conspirators.

General Cesare Amé, the tall, blue-eyed Piedmontese who was chief of Italy's Military Intelligence Service, Servizio Informazione Militaire (SIM), a close friend of Admiral Canaris, told the Admiral during the course of private discussions that Italy had to leave the war and that Il Duce must be overthrown. Canaris's reaction was sympathetic, perhaps because he thought the overthrow of Mussolini and the loss of Germany's valued ally might encourage German officers to follow the Italian example. But what occurred between late 1942 and 1943 was a zealous German Intelligence effort to uncover anti-Fascist conspiracies, during the course of which a number of other conspiracies, several involving the Abwehr, were discovered.

Gestapo and SD investigators pressed a meticulous enquiry, the anti-Mussolini movement became of secondary import-ance, and an Abwehr agent, Wilhelm Schmidhuber, a confidant of Canaris, was discovered to have smuggled Jews out of Germany into Switzerland in association with Hans von Dohnanyi of the Abwehr directorate.

While the Gestapo needed nothing more, it also discovered that Schmidhuber, a fat, coarse man, had also been involved indirectly with Josef Mueller's earlier secret negotiations at the Vatican when Pope Pius had agreed to contact British authorities for German dissidents.

Schmidhuber in fact knew a great deal, and when the Gestapo took him into custody, he got word to Canaris that unless the Admiral invoked Abwehr inviolability and got him out of the Prinzalbrechtstrasse dungeon, he would tell the Gestapo what he knew in exchange for liberty or, at the very least, for leniency.

Canaris, Oster and Dohnanyi met in secret session. Oster favoured an assassination – not very likely to succeed with Schmidhuber in the underground cells of Gestapo headquarters – and meanwhile Gestapo agents began the interrogation.

Schmidhuber, having heard nothing from Oster or his deputy Dohnanyi – who probably could not have got word to him by this time in any case – told his captors what he knew of the smuggling affair, and also about the Abwehr-Vatican connection. The more he revealed, the easier it became for astute Gestapo investigators to back-track and uncover additional evidence of Abwehr duplicity. A number of heretofore blind trails now led directly back to the Abwehr directorate. All the suspicion, all the Gestapo and SD intransigence which heretofore had languished for lack of solid evidence, was now being vindicated. For Military Intelligence the blows which were shortly to fall could be added to other recent calamities: despite Abwehr successes in Holland it had been deprived of the *England-Spiel* organization which had been transferred to the Gestapo's Funküberwachung. Then had come the successful commando raid at Bruneval after which an enraged Hitler had given counter-intelligence to Himmler's SD. What had heretofore been considered by the most charitable German critics of the Abwehr as inefficiency, now began to look like something quite different.

Schmidhuber's testimony drove a succession of nails into the

Abwehr's coffin. What had begun as a manhunt for anti-Fascists in Italy ended up in the Prinzalbrechtstrasse offices of the Gestapo, and three months after the first SD investigators appeared at Abwehr headquarters, Mussolini fell, dismissed by his king, taken into custody by the new Italian government of Marshal Badoglio, abandoned by the German secret agents who had been sent north to protect him from such eventualities.

Il Duce fell during the last week of July 1943. Earlier, in the first week of April, Commissioner Sonderegger (Kriminalkommissar, approximately 'Detective Superintendent') of the Gestapo, accompanied by Oberkriegsgerichtsrat (roughly, a legal assessor for military courts) Manfred Roeder, representing the judicial branch of Army administration (Reichskriegsgericht), entered the office of Admiral Canaris to announce that Hans von Dohnanyi was a British spy and that, along with his brother-in-law, the theologian Dietrich Bonhoeffer, Dohnanyi had been plotting, with assistance from the British secret services, to destroy Hitler and the German government.

Roeder had a warrant which he served, and over Canaris's protests Dohnanyi was arrested. He was taken to the Wehrmacht prison in Berlin. His superior, General Oster, was placed under house arrest. Josef Mueller and Dietrich Bonhoeffer were also taken into custody. The dragnet was spread wider. Himmler's SD, like wolves on a blood-trail, moved swiftly and relentlessly, but such was the nature of Intelligence work that, although Dohnanyi was charged with treason, he made an excellent case – as well he would, being by trade a lawyer – for all that he and others had done, as part of their normal espionage and counter-espionage work, and despite all that Schmidhuber had said, actual proof, particularly in writing, was lacking.

But Himmler was satisfied concerning Abwehr culpability and the personal involvement of Dohnanyi, Oster and Canaris. He was not disposed to allow the hearings to languish, especially when there was now such an excellent opportunity to destroy the Abwehr directorate and incorporate Military Intelligence into his own powerful security organization. However, external affairs were intruding even into the file rooms of men like Heinrich Himmler, whose lifelong preoccupation had been with compiling records, statistics and, over the past few years, secret dossiers on everyone including Adolf Hitler. The war was going very badly.

Then too, Admiral Canaris had not taken the assault on his aides with resignation. While Manfred Roeder was zealously pursuing his prosecution of Dohnanyi and others, the Admiral went to Field Marshal Keitel to complain that Roeder was trying to destroy the Abwehr's directorate for his own reasons of personal ambition, at a time when Military Intelligence was doing its utmost for the war effort. Keitel's reaction was to have Roeder re-assigned. His replacement, with Roeder's example before him, was quite willing to allow things to drift along. His job was not unpleasant, he was reasonably safe, and the alternative at this period was service at the Russian front.

But Manfred Roeder had been an army investigator. The behind-the-scenes battle had never been between the army and the Abwehr; it had been between the Abwehr and the Gestapo.

Dohnanyi, ailing by now, was sent to a hospital, and there the Gestapo appeared with authority to take him to an SS clinic where he was certified able to withstand an interrogation although barely able to stand unaided. SS or Gestapo interrogations rarely failed to achieve results, through either torture or fabrication. For Hans von Dohnanyi the final bend in the road was visible. He had a letter smuggled to his wife in which he said, 'The only thing to do is gain time. I must make certain that I am unfit to be tried.' She was to procure a diphtheria culture for him, which she did, and Dohnanyi developed the illness.

The exasperated Gestapo put an end to the charade by having the sick man taken out to a rubble heap where he was shot and killed.

For Canaris, his confidants and the Schwarze Kapelle, Dohnanyi's passing was one of a series of setbacks. Ludwig Beck, who had been a mainspring of the movement against Hitler for so long, had recently undergone surgery for the ailment which would have killed him if a bullet had not done it first. General Erwin Witzleben, another prominent conspirator, was suffering from aggravated haemorrhoids, and while there was younger blood coming up, such as the incredibly tough and dedicated Colonel Klaus Philip Maria Schenk,

Count von Stauffenberg – who would come closer than any
other to killing Hitler – the immediate need for a popular hero
to rally round came back to 'Kluger Hans' von Kluge, and now
more than ever it appeared that the Field Marshal might be
tempted. He had ended his inglorious months of doing nothing
by coming out in favour of the ill-fated *Fall Zitadelle* attack on
the Kursk salient and had influenced Hitler – whose procrastination foredoomed the campaign although it never had much
chance to succeed – in the face of fierce opposition from such
expert tacticians as Heinz Guderian and OKW Chief of Staff
Alfred Jodl.

The result was the greatest armoured battle in history,
during which the Germans lost 1,400 aircraft, 5,000 motor
vehicles, 1,000 guns, 3,000 tanks and 70,000 men in eleven
days. It was a worse defeat than Stalingrad had been. It
destroyed German initiative in the East. After *Zitadelle*, German arms followed the course of Bonaparte's walking dead of
1812.

Kluge's responsibility was partially obscured by simultaneous events elsewhere, in Italy, in Mediterrania, in rising
Europe, events which tended to confirm absolutely the demise
of German power.

For Guenther von Kluge a letter which reached him at this
time, from the same gaunt old conspirator he had met earlier,
Karl-Friedrich Goerdeler, suggested an alternative to retreat
and possibly ultimate disgrace as a defeated German general:
'The work of a thousand years is [now] nothing but rubble,'
the old man wrote, referring to the results of Allied air assaults
on Germany. 'In view of this national disaster . . . into which
we have been led by an insane and godless leadership . . . I take
the liberty of making a last appeal to you . . . The hour has now
come at which we must take the final decision on our personal
fate . . . German interests must . . . be represented with force
and reason by decent Germans.'

For von Kluge, surrounded by people he dared not trust, the
obvious course was the one he took. He replied to Goerdeler
simply and correctly; he was not interested.

Then he detached his Chief of Staff on an extended leave to
Berlin. This was the same General Henning von Tresckow who
had never stopped plotting against Hitler. Tresckow was to see

to it that the Schwarze Kapelle's conspiracy was properly organized along correct military lines. With von Tresckow went von Kluge's verbal promise to meet with leaders of the conspiracy when everything was in order.

In the late summer of 1943 a meeting was convened at the residence of Friedrich Olbricht, Chief of Staff of the Home Army under General Friedrich Fromm. Present were von Kluge, von Tresckow, Ludwig Beck and Goerdeler.

Kluge became committed. In the national interest, he said, Adolf Hitler must be overthrown. Finally, then, the conspiracy had a leader whose popularity and stature would ensure a rallying point for both civilians and soldiers.

But fate intervened as she had done so often. Back in Russia, Field Marshal von Kluge was seriously injured in an automobile collision near Minsk.

In Germany the weary conspirators started over again. General Erwin Witzleben was chosen to replace von Kluge. They also made some progress on a broad spectrum of problems including a fresh approach to the Allies, and again fate intervened.

Although a number of communications were sent to London outlining Schwarze Kapelle objectives and requesting acknowledgement of receipt along with appropriate comments, no reply was returned. An MI6 executive named Philby, called 'Kim' by his friends, made a point of intercepting and destroying communications from dissident Germans which might encourage a Nazi capitulation to the Western Allies before Philby's employer, the Soviet Union, could reach the Fatherland.

Other approaches, some to Britain, some to the Americans, some through neutral channels, were made without much success, although historians of those times suggested that the Schwarze Kapelle's endeavours did contribute to the war's end. In fact by the autumn of 1943 the war had long been lost, and by 1944 only a series of senseless, bloody campaigns remained to be endured by the people who, historically, went on sacrificing and dying long after there was any need for such anguish.

What the Schwarze Kapelle demonstrated was exactly what had been apparent from its beginning: that there were, in Goedeler's words, 'decent Germans' but that they lacked the capability to succeed, for whatever reasons, and they also seemed not to be the handmaidens of fate.

It may have been that the Devil did indeed look after his own. The Schwarze Kapelle not only consistently failed, but a majority of its protagonists died miserably as a result of their connection with it. But not all those who participated in attempts upon the life of Adolf Hitler belonged to the Schwarze Kapelle, and their lack of success was equally as noteworthy. Also, while Hitler was too perceptive not to appreciate the frailty of human nature and know he was surrounded by plotters and intriguists, he probably never suspected that among his personal entourage every single one had been approached at one time or another, including 'Treuer Heinrich' Himmler, Goering, Guderian, Goebbels, von Kluge, Rundstedt, Model, Rommel, the mostly American Baldur von Schirach, Schellenberg, Hess, *et al.*, and while all had rebuffed every suborning attempt – some, like Himmler, because they had their own plots in mind – not one of them had the dissidents arrested.

Between August and December 1943 five separate attempts were made on Hitler's life, but for various, in some cases eerie, reasons, none of them succeeded. Among the plotters one man, Dr Carl Langbehn, a co-conspirator with Heinrich Himmler, learned how icily indifferent friends became when an associate failed. Langbehn was uncovered by Walter Schellenberg, SD sub-chief under Himmler, was arrested, tried, condemned to death and sent to Mauthausen. Himmler intervened to protect his friend only to the extent of requiring through an intermediary that no one be allowed to attend Langbehn's trial or execution unless they were known to, and approved by, the Reichsführer himself. The SS then proceeded to execute Langbehn. First they terrified him, then they tortured him, and finally 'in a most barbarous and horrible manner' they tore off his genitals.

18

Lasciate ogni Speranza

At about this time the chief of station for the American Office of Strategic Services (OSS) in Switzerland, an old hand in the field of cloaks and daggers named Allen Dulles, summarized his knowledge of conditions inside the Third Reich in a report to Washington which included this sentence: 'The period of secret service under Canaris . . . is drawing to an end.'

He was correct. The process of whittling away had brought Canaris's organization to its lowest ebb, and both Dulles and the OSS helped the process.

Oster was gone, as was Dohnanyi; von Lahousen left the Abwehr for a field command – administrative colonels could only achieve general rank in this manner. Colonel Piekenbrock left for the same reason. Staff-Colonel von Bentivegni applied for field service too, but circumstances kept him with the organization until even Admiral Canaris was gone.

The Admiral had a few old confidants left, but not many, and he as well as they were now under constant surveillance, their telephones monitored, their guests and friends liable to persecution. Canaris had become a pariah, albeit a high-ranking one. The men who particularly wanted to destroy him, Walter Schellenberg, a chameleon-like younger man of great ambition, and his superior, Heydrich's successor as chief under Himmler of the SD, Ernst Kaltenbrunner, a bear of a man noted for sadistic brutality and marked by duelling scars, were restrained partly by Himmler and partly because Canaris, as a rear-admiral and a member of the German élite, was a dangerous adversary for subordinates to bait unless they could successfully impugn his character and create genuine doubts about his credibility, which was exactly what they were trying to do.

In their favour was the worsening political situation; Russia's army was pressing the offensive, Italy was leaving the war, a battered Wehrmacht was disintegrating from the bottom up, Nazi leadership had faltered almost to a standstill. The climate was ideal for jackals, and how subtly they worked was demonstrated when Canaris went to Venice for his last meeting with Cesare Amé. Schellenberg's spies had penetrated Amé's retinue so well that he was able to suborn two of the SIM chieftain's homosexual chauffeurs. They eavesdropped at the Venice meeting and reported to Schellenberg that both Amé and Canaris were deeply involved in treason – collaborating to get Italy out of the war – and not long afterward Cesare Amé was sent to command a combat division in the Balkans. His successor was General Carboni, who had once before headed Italian Military Intelligence.

Amé went into limbo. Canaris thought he had committed suicide. What became of him was an irrelevant mystery, but he did not appear at his duty station in the Balkans. After Italy's surrender, German officers said they had seen Amé in Venice. Perhaps, but it did not matter. What *did* matter was that someone had given Amé's superiors enough information concerning his connivance with Admiral Canaris to destroy him. The head of Italy's provisional government, Marshal Pietro Badoglio, over his head in a thicket of machiavellian intrigue, trusted no one, not even such a man as Cesare Amé who wanted the same things for Italy Badoglio wanted.

Canaris's enemies added the Amé affair to their dossier on the Admiral, some of which was seen by Hitler, probably through *Führertreuer* Himmler. By now the Führer's sanity was in question; his rages had become frightening and he saw enemies everywhere, as well he might.

But Military Intelligence still functioned professionally at most levels. Reliable reports still went to the High Generals. They were authentic, dependable and so chillingly accurate that Keitel rarely showed them to Hitler. The Abwehr, shortly to lose its head, had a body which would continue to writhe. Below the directorate level it remained efficient, dedicated and reliable. Only in its administration had it ceased to function as a professional Intelligence organization.

Schellenberg and Ernst Kaltenbrunner continued to whittle away while their superior, the Reichsführer, went about his personal schemes, the favourite of which was to protect an image of himself as the most reasonable – in fact as the only – alternative to Hitler, and he did it so surreptitiously that Hitler continued to believe that of all his entourage only Himmler was still completely loyal.

As Hitler had once said of the Soviet Union, one had only to kick in the door and the entire rotten structure would collapse. Now it would be Germany which would collapse, and with Russian armies approaching from the East and the 'Anglo-Americans' poised to strike through France, the period of time before someone kicked in the door was growing short.

By this time everyone in high positions knew that the conspiracy against Hitler abetted from within the Abwehr could not remain undisclosed much longer. Even Wilhelm Keitel, who screened most of what Hitler read, would have difficulties. Himmler for one leaked hints of high treason, and in Hitler's frame of mind many men had been put to death on less evidence. But with Germany on the defensive, finally, other things occupied the Führer's mind. He did not react characteristically – for a while.

Then, simultaneous events far beyond the shrinking borders of the Thousand-Year Reich triggered the explosion. In Turkey a lawyer (the Germans like the Americans seemed to favour lawyers in their clandestine work) named Paul Leverkuehn, headed the Abwehr facility. He had already come to Hitler's attention when in 1943 it was alleged that he and Franz von Papen, the German Ambassador at Ankara, had collaborated in support of peace-feelers. Leverkuehn was absolutely loyal to the Abwehr and Canaris, but not to Adolf Hitler. After the war he wrote a book, *German Military Intelligence* which was published in Britain, Germany and the US as 'A first-hand account of the Wehrmacht's Secret Service in the Second World War', in which he barely alluded, without names or details, to what actually occurred in his Ankara War Organization (KO) and which brought about Hitler's rage and resulted in Canaris's dismissal and the end of the Abwehr as an independent Intelligence organization.

Among Leverkuehn's agents in Turkey was a man named Erich Vermehren. When his wife, born a Countess Plettenberg, arrived at Ankara to be with her husband, she brought word of an investigation underway in Germany which might endanger

them both. She was known in the penetrated Catholic Resistance Movement in Germany, and the SD was investigating the
possibility that her husband had been in contact with the
British.

Erich Vermehren reacted predictably, and with excellent
reasons. He was in fact a double agent known in British
Intelligence circles as 'Junior'. It was the spring of 1944. Both
the Vermehrens invoked their Last Resort, the signal of alarm,
and were clandestinely picked up by a British aeroplane and
flown to safety in Cairo. After their defection the SD accused
them of absconding with top-secret documents.

In Berlin the Vermehrens' defection created quite a stir in the
Intelligence community. Schellenberg and Kaltenbrunner took
fullest advantage of it in their campaign against the Abwehr.

Then another pair of Abwehr-Ankara agents defected, a
man and his wife named either von Kletschowsky or Klecy-
kowski, both of whom had held sensitive posts in Leverkuehn's organization for several years. These events were
followed in quick succession by the defection of the secretary
of the Gestapo attaché in Ankara who sought, and was
granted, sanctuary in the American embassy, and other
Abwehr defections in Portugal, Sweden and North Africa.

These affairs 'aroused Hitler to a pitch of frenzy and fury
rare even for him'. He blamed Paul Leverkuehn more than the
defectors, calling Leverkuehn 'a typical Canaris man', and was
reported to have said that Canaris 'was directly responsible
that this filthy mess had not been prevented'.

He then sent for Himmler and ordered him immediately to
undertake the creation of one unified Intelligence organization. General Alfred Jodl telephoned Field Marshal Keitel with
this decision, and Keitel called Canaris to inform him that the
Abwehr was now to be incorporated into Himmler's RSHA.

Schellenberg and Kaltenbrunner wasted no time. Through
Himmler a directive was submitted for Hitler's signature
which formally announced that henceforth there would be 'a
single German Secret Intelligence Service [and that] . . . the
direction of this Service [is to be under] . . . the Reichsführer
SS . . .'.

These events, coming abruptly from a direction Canaris
certainly had not expected, were nevertheless not a complete

surprise. The toady twins Keitel and Jodl motored to Zossen, where the Abwehr headquarters had been relocated sometime earlier, for a conference with Admiral Canaris. He was, they said, to take leave, and when he returned he would be director of the Department of Economic Warfare at Eiche near Potsdam. He was also given a decoration. Himmler clearly was not after his head, although Ernst Kaltenbrunner was. As for Walter Schellenberg, once Canaris had been dismissed, his organization to become part of the RSHA, his interest atrophied, for a time anyway.

For Canaris, however, the end, which probably should have been a relief, was not, although the transition was made bearable by something – disillusionment, age (he was 57 in 1944), exhaustion, too many failures or just plain resignation. He was no longer in the mainstream. The Schwarze Kapelle, while still active, had passed into the hands of younger men. He had little to do with it after 1944. There were still contacts, but direct participation had not been provided by the Admiral or his former associates since the autumn before.

The Abwehr now became Amt Mil, Walter Schellenberg's new military organization, part of Himmler's total security and Intelligence system. Replacing Canaris as the subordinate head of Military Intelligence was Colonel Georg Hansen, the last head of Abwehr I. He was both an active member of the Schwarze Kapelle and a Canaris disciple, but for a long time neither Schellenberg nor Kaltenbrunner suspected it.

One of the results of the Abwehr's destruction and reorganization was that, with disaster approaching from all sides, the eyes of Military Intelligence were temporarily blinded. In the field Abwehr agents, unsure of their future and subjected to a blizzard of conflicting directives, suffered from demoralization and confusion. Another result was that the Allies were able to launch a number of successful deceptions against Germany which might have succeeded anyway but which were certainly not hindered by the disarray in Germany's Military Intelligence community.

Admiral Canaris took up his duties at Eiche. There was no reason for enthusiasm; economic warfare had never been one of Nazi Germany's more vigorous programmes. He was still under surveillance, his telephones were monitored, his mail was censored, and his contacts were watched and investigated. Under the circumstances even old acquaintances among the dissident groups did not look forward to his visits, nor did he make many such calls.

His family was now in Bavaria, a move made necessary as a result of daily Allied air raids. The house at Schlachtensee was lonely, even though he had two servants and among the neighbours he had several close friends.

In the afternoon of 20 July 1944 he received a telephone call informing him that the Führer was dead, killed by a bomb. This referred to the Stauffenberg plot, of which he had knowledge but of which he had thought little, since, this close to Armageddon, Hitler's passing would be anticlimactic.

At 5 p.m. on 20 July, a call came from Berlin informing the Admiral that Hitler was not dead, that again he had survived an attempt on his life. Of course both these calls were monitored, and in the backlash of violence which ensued, people were taken into custody by the hundreds, including those who had received telephone calls about the attempt on the day it happened.

On the pleasant Sunday afternoon of 23 July 1944 SS-Standartenführer Walter Schellenberg drove up to the house in Schlachtensee in the company of an associate, SS-Hauptstürmführer Baron von Voelkersham. Canaris met them at the doorstep. To Schellenberg he said, 'Somehow I felt it would be you. Please come in.'

Schellenberg was civil, almost sympathetic. But his orders were to arrest Canaris, and he obeyed them. As they were walking out to the car, Canaris said, 'It is too bad we have to say good-bye in this way.'

He was taken to the Prinzalbrechstrasse SD headquarters and put into one of the underground cells.

He was questioned, but without abuse, and he was quartered in a separate, rather comfortable cell. Here he discovered how sweeping had been the purge after the attempt on Hitler's life. Also in the dungeon were Karl-Friedrich Goerdeler, Herbert Goering (Reichsmarschall Herman Goering's cousin), General Halder, Pastor Bonhoeffer, General Thomas and Canaris's acolyte of better times, Colonel – now General – Hans Oster, along with Dr Hjalmar Schacht and Josef Mueller, plus a dozen others, some, like Dr Schacht, former high officials of the government.

The interrogations continued, and as the Admiral held his own, his treatment became more harsh. He was given a third of normal rations, was compelled to wear chains and was put to such work as cleaning filth-encrusted execution cells. On 2 February 1945 Goerdeler was taken to the yard and shot to death. The following day, the 3rd, during the course of an Allied saturation bombing the Gestapo building was destroyed, but the underground area remained usable although there was no longer running water to flush the latrines or to wash in, so its over-crowded condition was somewhat alleviated with the removal of a number of prisoners, including Canaris to the SS Flossenburg camp near Weiden in Bavaria's upper Palatinate.

Here there were no pretences. No one was expected to leave alive and very few did. The interrogations were resumed, but not zealously; no one was required to confess to anything, for no one was going to live long enough for confessions to matter. With or without certified affidavits, the sentence would be the same.

The methods of torture at Flossenburg as at other concentration camps had been refined from years of experience. Admiral Canaris's cell, for example, was purposefully over-heated, and he slept on a wooden bunk, forbidden to lie in any position but on his back, chained. At the foot of the bunk a high-intensity white electric light was kept burning throughout the night. Interrogations were brutal. At one point the Admiral's nose was broken and several of his teeth were knocked out.

As von Dohnanyi had written to his wife, the objective was to gain time, and in the spring of 1945 it seemed that such a course might prevail, but that was because prisoners like Admiral Canaris had no knowledge of orders to make certain no prisoner who was able to chronicle Nazi excesses would be alive when the advancing Allies arrived.

Among the captives was H. M. Lunding, formerly a Lieutenant-Colonel of Danish Military Intelligence. His cell, Number 21, offered a view through cracks in the door of the execution area. the cell was seventy yards away, and during

Lunding's ten months residence at Flossenburg he had attempted to tally the executions. The number was close to nine hundred.

On the evening of 8 April 1945, twenty-nine days before Germany's surrender ended the war in Europe, and with the Americans only about eighty-five miles away, Admiral Canaris was put on trial before an SS Standgericht (summary court) charged with high treason. Both he and Hans Oster were sentenced to death. Oster was executed before dawn the following morning. Canaris was returned to his cell after the sentencing, where he tapped out a message to Colonel Lunding using a spoon on a water pipe. It ended with: 'Do what you can for my wife and daughters. They have broken my nose. I die this morning. Farewell.'

The guards arrived at daybreak. Canaris was taken naked to the yard without his chains, and although it was customary to shoot officers rather than to strangle them, Canaris was hanged from the courtyard rafters by an iron collar. When he was taken down presumed dead, and found to be still alive, he was hoisted up again. It took him thirty minutes to die.

His body was burned and the ashes were dumped in a pit of ashes from other executions.

A month later the German war was over. Hitler was dead. Goering and Himmler shortly would be, by suicide, and Canaris's particular nemesis, Ernst Kaltenbrunner, along with Alfred Jodl, Wilhelm Keitel and others, was put to death after the Nuremburg War Crimes Trials. Walter Schellenberg became of use to the Americans and died of a liver ailment in 1950.

Not many Germans who had known Admiral Canaris in their official capacities died in bed. Schellenberg used the five years left to him after the war to exonerate himself, as did other former high Germans such as Albert Speer, Hitler's particular favourite, who managed to do it so well that he emerged with the sympathy of his former enemies without deserving any of it.

Bibliography

The most important published sources in the preparation of this book are the following:

Paul W. Blackstock, *World War II* (Quadrangle Books, Chicago, 1969). A good source for Intelligence machinations up to World War Two.

Anthony Cave Brown, *Bodyguard of Life* (Bantam Books, New York and London, 1975). An outstanding source for Intelligence aspects of World War Two.

Winston Churchill, *The Second World War* Houghton Mifflin, Boston, 1948).

E. H. Cookbridge, *Set Europe Ablaze* (Thomas Y. Crowell, New York, 1967).

Dwight D. Eisenhower, *Crusade in Europe* (Doubleday, New York, 1948). Not a book on Intelligence sources, but exemplary for verification of names, dates, events and places.

Walter Goerlitz, *The German General Staff* (orig. *Der Deutsche Generalstab*, Verlag der Frankfurter Hefte. Praeger, New York, 1953). The most scholarly, thorough, and readable book on the great General Staff presently available. A good secondary source on German Intelligence.

Adolf Hitler, *Mein Kampf* (Reynaud and Hitchcock, New York, 1939). Usable in connection with any study of German World War Two Intelligence.

Paul Leverkuehn, *German Military Intelligence* (Praeger, New York, 1945). Leverkuehn was an Abwehr station chief in Turkey.

Harry and Bonaro Overstreet, *The War Called Peace* (W. W. Norton, New York, 1961).

Günter Peis and Charles Wighton, *Hitler's Spies and Saboteurs* (Henry Holt, New York, 1958). Based on the Abwehr diary of General von Lahousen.

H. R. Trevor-Roper, *The Last Days of Hitler* (Macmillan, London and New York, 1947).

F. W. Winterbotham, *The Ultra Secret* (Harper & Row, New York and London, 1974). Despite sebsequent publications on the subject of the cipher war, Frederick Winterbotham's book remains pre-eminent.

Also consulted:

Karl-Heinz Adshagen, *Canaris* (Hutchinson, London, 1956).

Karl Bartz, *The Downfall of the German Secret Service* (W. Kimber, London, 1956).

S. Payne Best, *The Venlo Incident* (Hutchinson, London, 1950).

Paul W. Blackstock, *Agents of Deceit* (Quadrangle Books, Chicago, 1966).

Alan Bullock, *Hitler* (Bantam Books, New York, 1953).

Allan Chase, *Falange* (G. P. Putnams' Sons, New York, 1943). Contains interesting information on German penetration of *Ausland* societies.

Alan Clark, *Barbarossa* (William Morrow, New York, 1965).

E. H. Cookbridge, *Inside S.O.E.* (Barker, London, 1966).

Edward Crankshaw, *Gestapo* (Pyramid Books, New York, 1945).

Allen W. Dulles, *The Craft of Intelligence* (Harper & Row, New York, 1963).

Allen W. Dulles, *Germany's Underground* (Macmillan, New York, 1947).

Ladislas Farago, *The Game of Foxes* (D. McKay, New York, 1971).

Reinhard Gehlen, *The Service* (World Publishing Company, New York, 1972).

Felix Gilbert, *Hitler Directs His War* (Oxford University Press, New York, 1950).

Hermann J. Giskes, *London calling North Pole* (W. Kimber, London, 1953).

Eugen Kogon, *The Theory and Practice of Hell* (Berkley, New York, 1950).

William L. Langer, *An Encyclopaedia of World History* (Houghton Mifflin, New York, 1952).

J. De Launay, *European Resistance Movements* (Pergamon Books, London, 1960).

Lord Russell of Liverpool, *The Scourge of the Swastika* (Ballantine Books, New York, 1954).

Peter Way, *Codes and Ciphers* (Crown Books, New York, 1977).

Additional sources of information, quite often indirect but nonetheless pertinent, include:

W. F. Flicke, *Die Rote Kapelle* (Hilden, Rhein, Germany, 1949).

J. O. Fuller, *The German Penetration of S.O.E.* (Kimber Company, New York, 1975). This is worth reading as a counterweight to Cookbridge's book.

Reinhard Gehlen, *The Service: The memoirs of General Reinhard Gehlen* (Popular Library, New York, 1972).

H. Höhne and H. Zolling, *The General was a Spy: The truth about General Gehlen and his spy ring* (Coward, McCann, Geoghegen, New York, 1971).

W. Hoettl, *The Secret Front: the story of Nazi political espionage* (Weidenfeld and Nicolson, London, 1953).

D. Irving, *The German Atom Bomb* (Simon & Schuster, New York, 1968).

David Kahn, *The Codebreakers* (Macmillan, New York 1967).

Wilhelm Keitel, *The Memoirs of Field Marshal Keitel* (Stein & Day, New York, 1966). This posthumously published story of Feldmarschall Wilhelm Keitel who was with Hitler from the early days and who was also in the Bunker with him is, I believe, a far more straightforward presentation than Albert Speer's apologia.

H. Manvell, *Himmler* (Ediciones Grijalbo, Barcelona, 1972).

Albert Speer, *Inside the Third Reich: The memoirs of Albert Speer* (Macmillan, New York, 1970).

K. W. D. Strong, *Intelligence at the Top: Recollections of an Intelligence Officer* (Doubleday, New York, 1968).

J. G. Weiner, *The Assassination of Heydrich* (Grossmuller, New York, 1969).

INDEX

Index